SEND
BETTER
EMAILS

Jon May

Softback version ISBN 978-1-913713-44-7
Limited hardback version ISBN 978-1-913713-22-5

Published by Compass-Publishing UK

Edited and designed by The Book Refinery Ltd
www.thebookrefinery.com

A catalogue copy of this book is available from the British Library.

Printed and bound in the UK

Dedicated to your email subscribers.
May this book help you Send Better Emails *to them.*

CONTENTS

Foreword 9

Introduction 11

Who is this book for? 11

What is email marketing? 12

How does marketing via email work? 13

THE TEN EMAIL COMMANDMENTS 15

The email jigsaw 16

How to read this book 18

Example Company Ltd. 19

PDF downloads – Resources for the Reader 19

The Ten Email Commandments 21

1. Treat readers as royalty 21

2. Ask permission 22

3. Be honest 23

4. Let go (gracefully) 27

5. Keep data safe 31

6. Build relationships 32

7. Work smarter 33

8. Get planning 34

9. Keep going 35

10. Send Better Emails 35

SECTION ONE – BUILD A STRATEGY – 37

Chapter 1: How can I help? 39

What value can you add to the reader? 39

Help a narrow niche 41

Give more than you take 42

Chapter 2: Planning emails..43

Reader persona...43

The path to fandom...47

The one-page email brief...51

The automation sequences every business needs..........54

Chapter 3: Defining success..56

Action-based planning..56

Be clear about what you want...60

Make buttons great again..60

Use active language...62

Be immediate..63

The business metrics for success..................................63

Average Order Value..64

Customer Lifetime Value...65

Email metrics...68

Open rates...71

Click rates...81

SECTION TWO – GROW YOUR AUDIENCE - 87

Chapter 4: Signing up..89

How to say hi......91

1. Lead magnet – where they get a thing, then a newsletter. 92

2. Newsletter IS the magnet..92

Set expectations...96

Single opt-in...99

Pop ups...99

Tracking people 103

Easy to leave..104

Chapter 5: Saying hello...105

What is a welcome sequence?...105
Why welcome sequences work...106
Offer value not discounts..106

Welcome sequence templates...111

Chapter 6: Promoting your list..115

Putting people off..115
Ask questions – does this sound like you?...116

Keeping up with the Joneses..117
Where do your readers hang out?...117
Promoting through partnerships...119
Business partnerships...119

Targeting the competition..121
Roping in your existing clients...122

SECTION THREE – CONVERT MORE READERS – 125

Chapter 7: Why data is king..127

What data do I need?...127
How are you protecting it?...129

Better passwords...129
Increased security..131

What extra data do you collect?...132
How do I manage all my lists?...133
Group/segment people to create many lists within one.....................135
Trim regularly..135

Chapter 8: Working Smarter...142

Segmentation..142
Personalisation...145

Image personalisation 153

How to set up image personalisation 155

Data-led automated emails 157

Chapter 9: What's next? 166

Getting the sequence right 166

Abandoned basket 167

What's the post-purchase experience? 170

Receipt 174

The delivery notification/gap 179

Review/feedback 184

Follow up (Did everything arrive OK?) 186

Care/usage instructions 186

Cross sells and upsells (You might like...) 189

Replenishment reminder 191

Refer a friend 191

Loyalty scheme/VIP membership club 193

Onboarding 195

Non-recent customers 200

Putting it all together 203

Starting from zero 203

Pick your platform 204

Data 205

E-commerce 206

Creating a newsletter 206

The post-purchase experience 214

The last thought 216

Glossary 217

Reference 219

About the author 220

Acknowledgements 221

Foreword

The death of email marketing has been greatly exaggerated. It's very much alive and kicking, especially if you *Send Better Emails*.

As a Chief Marketing Officer working for an iconic UK brand, and in my years of working in marketing, I've learned that cutting corners or trying to find the "magic bullet" is, unfortunately, never going to be the answer.

I've been lucky enough to work for many different organisations, with many strong marketeers, and the answer is always continuous improvement through ongoing optimisation.

And that couldn't be truer in email marketing – whether that's through building and nurturing your email list, driving consumer engagement or converting to sales – it's all about incremental, and often marginal, gains.

The marketing mix and how email fits into this has changed over time. Consumer expectations and behaviour, marketing technology and, most importantly, data regulation have had a profound impact on the topic.

In the early part of my career, I recall email as a cheap alternative to direct mail and an easy way to buy access to large customer prospect lists with dubious provenance. Now, email is a highly regulated but hugely valuable cornerstone for any marketing campaign. It's a way to create vibrant conversations and drive real-time results that anyone can master with the right approach. Moreover, it doesn't require deep pockets.

Email marketing can work for every business and, as an owned rather than paid media channel, it can be built from scratch and developed to give a real advantage. In short, it's democratised direct marketing with low costs and real-time results. It's also relevant whether your business goal is to acquire new customers or increase the engagement, loyalty and value of those you already have.

Technology and the automation and personalisation this can bring are essential. Still, email is nothing without data – whether that's the email list itself or the information you hold that can genuinely turn your email activity into something out of the ordinary and a legitimately engaging conversation with your audience. The trick is knowing how to do this.

I am lucky enough to work with Jon, and he has taken our email marketing to the next level (and it was pretty formidable already!). He knows what he's doing, and you'll feel this as you read his book. This isn't dry marketing theory, it's gold dust based on real experiences, from small businesses through to big brand campaign activity.

Jon's incredibly customer-centric, and he has balanced the longer game of loyalty building through engagement with commercial sales performance to provide a truly sustainable and scalable channel.

Through his clear and simple processes and guidance, he's also brought the structure, leadership and mindset required to make email marketing a critical and successful ingredient in the overall marketing mix.

Read the chapters attentively, go over the words, follow the email jigsaw framework and give it a go.

This is a medium where you are in control and not beholden to the black-box techniques and costs that underpin some other media.

With *Send Better Emails* by your side, you'll have all the advantages that big brands and big budgets enjoy.

Alex Heath, Chief Customer and Marketing Officer, RAC

Introduction

Who is this book for?

If you're wondering how to improve your emails, or even where to start, you're in the right place.

From getting a plan together, growing a list, nailing down some awesome welcome sequences and automations, through to converting readers into customers, this book looks at the whole reader journey and how each piece of the email puzzle fits in to help you *Send Better Emails*.

If you're just getting started, the last chapter, *Putting it All Together*, focuses on how to get up and running from scratch.

This book will help you to clarify where you are on your email journey, providing a roadmap of where you want to be and which areas you might need to focus on.

I wrote this book for the amazing and creative business owners who've had the courage to strike out on their own and are experts at what they do, whether that's accountancy, HR, marketing . . . the list goes on. They are brilliant and bright minds in their field, but they struggle to get email up and running and to see the returns from their investment of time and resources in sending emails that convert well.

Every brand I've worked with has wanted to make more money (or to start making money) with email marketing. And it's definitely possible. There's always something else you can do to improve it – no email is perfect. Every single marketing email I send out, whether it's on behalf of a client or for my own business, could be made better.

That headline could be a bit shorter, that button could be a bit snappier, that code could be a bit more efficient. But perfection is the enemy of done, so I always try and improve one aspect in every iteration, see how it performs and then add (or ignore) that test moving forward.

This means I'm always learning and growing, and, more importantly, the readers are constantly getting the best email, based on evidence and experimentation. And that's what I want for you – to look at what you're doing now and have a go at making a few small tweaks.

You'll be surprised at how tiny changes can lead to big results. In a recent campaign, I changed the text on the main button to be a bit more action focused, and the email gained an additional £8k in revenue. Just changing it up and tweaking three words added these extra sales – and it didn't cost a penny.

But if just writing a few emails and blasting them out was all there was to it, we'd all be millionaires, right?

There's always a bit of luck, a dash of gut feeling and a sprinkling of "done is better than perfect". (Which, incidentally, is why this book is called *Send Better Emails* rather than *Plan Perfect Emails*!)

What is email marketing?

I was at a party shortly after the big General Data Protection Regulations (GDPR) blitz of 2018, and someone asked me what I do. After learning I helped brands with their email marketing, they joked, "So, you're the reason I get so many spammy emails!" And that's a fair representation of what comes to most people's minds when they think about email marketing.

Even post GDPR, emails get a bad rep. They can be invasive, spammy and seek to only serve the company not the customer. *But it doesn't have to be this way.*

It could be a conversation. It could be a nugget of useful information. It could be a link to a funny video. Whatever's inside the email, you're making use of a unique channel that is incredibly effective, but it should try to help the reader. That could be through providing a connection, something to make them laugh or something that inspires them.

No matter how big or small you are, email is cheap in comparison to paid digital advertising, and it can really bring home the bacon.

I always suggest a ratio of three 'helpful' emails to every promotional one. What makes a helpful email? Anything that helps someone solve a problem that doesn't include money changing hands.

Products can be useful (they always should be!), but the willingness to show you care is more important to people than an extravagantly designed email with a big Buy Now button.

In this book, I'm going to explain exactly how you can build, grow and convert readers in an honest, natural way that sets up a longer relationship for the future, not just the archaic "batch and blast" for a quick buck.

How does marketing via email work?

Marketing is persuading someone to do something. Email is just the channel or medium in which you do it. Others include social media or billboards.

Email is not Facebook and it's not Twitter. You shouldn't just try to copy and paste the marketing messages you put on other channels and blast them out – I've seen this done a few times and it bombs.

When I get an email, I have to read who it's from, the subject line and the preview text, but I don't have to open it and I don't have to click on anything if I do.

When a reader gets your email, it interrupts their day. They're waiting for the bus, they're on the loo, they're checking their inbox as the kettle boils. You have to make it worth their while for the interruption, for the privilege of the open and the click.

Readers don't need emails in their life. It's your job to make them need *your* emails. You need to deliver so much help, advice and value to their problem that when they get your email they go, "Ooh, I need to sit down to read this one properly."

Email marketing is more than just coupons and e-commerce, it's building a connection with the person on the other end of the mailbox to develop a long-term relationship.

Whether you're selling infrequent high-ticket items (like cars, beds or kitchens) or are geared more towards the consumable end (like books, cosmetics or drinks), building a connection is important for the repeat business.

And it's the follow-up that really is the measure of a brand's email process.

→ *Once they've bought from you, do they still get promotional messages?*

→ *Do they get the same newsletter, but without the adverts or promos for the product they've already bought?*

→ *Once a reader subscribes, do they get a welcome sequence?*

I talk about this more in Section Two – Chapter 5: *Saying Hello*, with some quick wins for you to get set up and started with.

THE TEN EMAIL COMMANDMENTS

There are ten basic principles that should be the solid foundation of everything you do. Whenever you're thinking about emails, keep these in mind. (I go into more detail about each of these starting on page 21.)

1. **Treat readers as royalty**

    Your readers are the judge, jury and executioner of your email campaigns. If they don't like them, you'll get a stony silence.

2. **Ask permission**

    It's so basic to ask someone before you add them to a mailing list, and yet you'd be surprised how many list companies are still selling data.

3. **Be honest**

    Deliver on what you promise – "Free product" in a subject line that's actually a Buy One Get One Free might be a bit misleading. A lot of these shouldn't be controversial, just the basics of operating a business.

4. **Let go (gracefully)**

    Let people unsubscribe easily, quickly and gracefully. No bullying or guilt tripping with, "BUT YOU'LL MISS OUT ON OUR OFFERS!"

5. **Keep data safe**

    If you're using an email platform, this one's covered, but always ensure that when people give you their data, it's safe and secure.

6. **Build relationships**

    Building relationships is buying the first round at the pub – people will be grateful, and you'll reap the rewards later. Don't be that guy who enjoys the evening but disappears just before their turn.

7. **Work smarter**

   Why do twice as much work? Setting up automations is a massive time saver and will help most of your emails run on autopilot.

8. **Get planning**

   Emails are like icebergs – customers see the email in their inbox, but the hard work of preparing the content, designing an eye-catching layout and collecting and sorting data is the 90% of the ice that is under the water.

9. **Keep going**

   Set a schedule for sending out emails and stick to it. Build up a few in reserve for when life gets a bit much.

10. **Send Better Emails**

    Always look at how you might tweak something. Even moving the needle 1% every week with tiny tweaks moves the collective needle 52% a year.

The email jigsaw

As I started to specialise in email marketing, I saw the same things appearing in successful campaigns. These were always the same, no matter the technology used to create them, the product or the offer.

Brands are always in one of four stages of their journey:

1. **Building a strategy** – (this is in Section One – *Build A Strategy*)

2. **Growing their list** – (this is in Section Two – *Grow Your List*)

3. **Converting readers to customers** – (this is in Section Three – *Convert More Readers*)

4. **Putting theory into practice** – (this is in the last chapter, *Putting it All Together*)

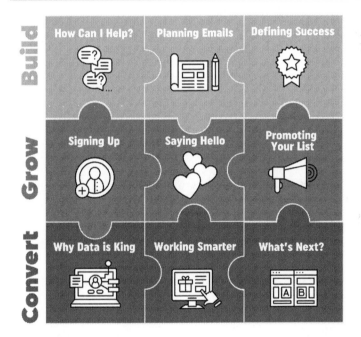

While I was collecting these important factors that I could see were moving the needle in well-performing campaigns and helping businesses to grow their revenue, I created the Email Jigsaw, a clear roadmap for success.

It became apparent that using and connecting each piece was needed for the best possible outcome and the highest-performing campaigns.

If you're just starting out, focus on growing your list and look more seriously at conversions a little later, when you've got more people (and more data) to look at.

If you either haven't sent any emails at all or for at least six months, you should start at the beginning and work your way up to conversions. Don't get disheartened if you send out an email and don't get any sales. This isn't one of those "10x your business with growth hacks" – this is a commitment to doing it properly, so that you get steady and sustainable long-term revenue from your email list.

How to read this book

Personally, I'd read it all the way through – perhaps putting some sticky notes on the areas you know you'll want to work on further, before going back afterwards.

As it's a jigsaw, all the pieces are important, but I often find that people want to get stuck in and jump into sending emails out, when the rest of the plan is missing. This is a mistake, because a lot of the advice in one chapter flows into the next. It's only a picture when you step back and see how it all works together.

Especially within the *Build, Grow* and *Convert* sections, a lot of what might be talked about in one area will be looked back at in another, so I'd advise against jumping straight in, as you might miss some of the finer points of the big picture.

Each piece of the puzzle builds on the last and sets up the next.

If you prefer a bit of chaos, read it backwards!

Example Company Ltd

While these strategies will apply in some shape to all businesses, it's a bit easier for me to pin them to one example company, so you can see how that might translate to your business.

I'm a bit of an indoor plant nut. My house is covered in plants and I've actually received some really nice comments from clients who've enjoyed my plant display as a background on video calls. I can't close some of my doors because plants are hanging off them. I'm not doing too bad a job – most of them are still alive! I've got an app that reminds me when to water them (the amazing Hedira app was founded by my friend Jess Samaurez).

On this theme, and to demonstrate how to use emails, I thought I'd set up a (fake) high-street retailer called **Poppy's Plants**. They've got a website to buy plants and there are some gardening services attached to it, in addition to a service renting out larger plants with care packages.

That should be a good grounding to cover retail, e-commerce, B2B (business to business) and B2C (business to consumer) services. As we go through examples of different concepts, I'll keep bringing it back to Poppy's Plants and how the concepts might link into it, so you can see a real-life scenario.

Any resemblance to any company or business is purely coincidental; I just liked the alliteration of Poppy's Plants.

PDF downloads – Resources for the Reader

You can download all the resources, including reader personas and flowcharts, featured in this book at sendbetter.email/resources.

Here, you'll find all the examples, templates and guides I've talked about, from the email brief to the one-page plan. You can download them, print them out and fill in the PDFs at your own pace.

The Ten Email Commandments

Here, I'll go through the *Ten Email Commandments* in more detail, although I could par them down into a concise, "Don't be a dick."

Most of these commandments are unlikely to rustle the feathers of any email marketer; they are all key tenets of good emails and you'll see them in various versions from other email experts.

1. Treat readers as royalty

It still surprises me when I see marketing emails that are clearly solely for the business, with no regard for the reader. Without the reader, the business is nothing. Without the business, the reader won't even notice.

Treating the reader as the royalty they are, recognises that it's a two-way relationship, but also that the reader is the magnanimous emperor, deciding which way to point their thumb in the gladiatorial arena of the inbox.

Readers are always giving you feedback. Whether through sales and revenue or with an unsubscribe, they do this without saying a word. Using metrics to track positive and negative engagements can highlight problems before they snowball.

Your readers wear the crown. They are the judge, jury and executioner to your offer and your email. They run the world that you are encroaching on.

Treat royalty as peasants at your own risk. Justice is swift, and they won't hesitate to reach for the guillotine and leave your email list forever.

Try not to fall into the trap of, "I need to email everyone on my list, every time with every offer, because they all *need* my product!" Instead, look at ways to tailor the email to the specific pain point the reader might be experiencing (and that hopefully you have a solution for).

Whether readers themselves think they need that product is only evidenced in the conversion rate of an email. If the results are bad, don't blame the readers. Work out what went wrong and *send a better email.*

2. Ask permission

In May 2018, you'll remember learning about a new data protection law, GDPR, only because your inbox was overloaded with pleas from businesses desperate to keep sending you emails.

The new law means you have to ask people to sign up to your list before sending them anything, and if only brands had done that all along, the avalanche of emails could have been abated. There are a few other things that are important, but the idea of explicit consent is key.

To email someone with marketing content, you need *explicit* consent. That means they have to be screaming, *When Harry Met Sally*-style, "YES! RIGHT IN MY INBOX! I WANT TO GET YOUR EMAILS!"

But just like being in someone's house, consent isn't permanent.

If one of your recipients hasn't opened any of your emails in six months, it's likely they don't want to hear from you. Whether that's because they're now uninterested (like getting estate agents' listings after buying a house), or they're no longer around (moved job, got married and changed their name, or died) – they're no longer a prospective customer and you should try to win them back. Then, if they still don't signal that they want to know, it's time to automatically unsubscribe them.

This helps you in two ways: more of your emails get delivered because all the bad numbers (bounce, unsubscribes, non-openers) go down and all the good numbers (open rate, clicks, engagement) go up.

Imagine sending your emails is like going out for a coffee with a subscriber. You wouldn't (I hope!) say hello and forcibly pour hot coffee down their throat.

You'd ask them if they wanted a coffee and, depending on their answer, you'd either get them one or not. It'd be weird to buy a coffee for someone who didn't ask for one, and also to keep talking to them if their coffee went cold.

© marketoonist.com

3. Be honest

For me, honesty is just a basic prerequisite for every aspect of life. This isn't a philosophical debate on social lies (like, "Yes, you look great in that!"), it's more about the promises a brand makes that then need to be followed through.

Again, none of these things should be controversial.

"Enter your email and download this guide on problem X" should mean they receive a download of that guide.

"Sign up for £15 off your first order" should mean you get a £15 off coupon. Again, it's straightforward, and when this doesn't work it's either the tech or because someone forgot to check it, rather than a more dishonest bait-and-switch of, "Give me your email address for a prize, but the joke's on you, as there isn't one."

All pretty straightforward so far.

But omitting what signing up really means can be dishonest, too.

Like, "Sign up for £15 off your first order", but leaving out that they'll hound you into an early grave, or that you'll finish up crafting a new identity just to escape the two or three emails a day if you don't buy (and even more if you do).

Setting those expectations of, "Download this guide and we'll send you a weekly roundup about problem X" really helps the reader understand what they're getting into.

A great example of combining an offer with a download comes from RippedBody.com (a site I probably ought to use more to achieve a less well-rounded marketing consultant look!).

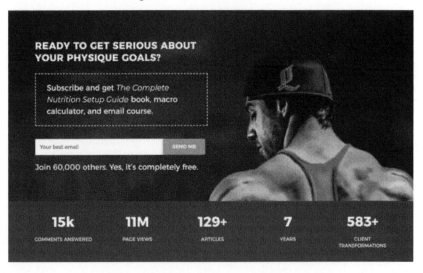

Example 1 – Screenshot of a popup from RippedBody.com.

The way it combines the question: "Ready to get serious about your physique goals?" as well as the free things you get after subscribing, in addition to the social proof that 60k others have done so, makes it seem like a no-brainer.

This kind of opt-in on a website homepage converts incredibly highly for motivated readers.

The number of subscribers is just typed into the popup or sign-up page, it's very rarely anything technical. Every now and again, when you pass a big benchmark, update it and it'll boost that social proof.

When you're starting out, it might be a bit disheartening to write, "Join 2 other people on my list (me and my mum!)", but when you get past two digits, or a number you're not embarrassed by, it can help people who are sitting on the fence by letting them know that other people have found it useful.

Social proof can be incredibly compelling, and it doesn't have to be numbers, it can also involve what other people think about signing up.

Take a look at this example from the marketing agency Spaghetti:

Example 2 – Sign-up form at marketing agency Spaghetti.

While they've included a more generic "Join 1,000s of raving fans", right underneath this there is feedback solicited from their 'Friday Digital Roundup', a curated list of funny stories from the internet that week.

Learning what other people think about something can be a powerful way to encourage our reader to sign up. Just look at how highly Google thinks of reviews and how big of a deal Trustpilot is to companies that rely and depend on it.

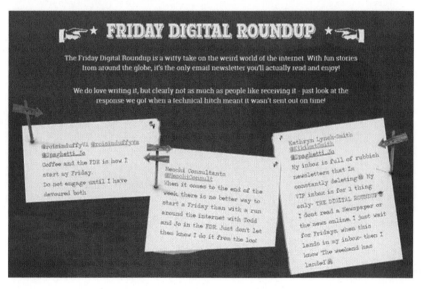

Example 3 – Social proof from the Friday Digital Roundup newsletter.

The more commercially minded of you might think, "That doesn't sound very valuable", but it's all about offering a bit of a chuckle on a Friday morning, with the occasional advert for their services thrown in.

It demonstrates they've got a pulse on the things that happen online, which appeals to people who don't. And it reminds the reader that the agency is available for hire to fill in that gap for their business.

When you're starting out, start simple. Something like, "Join other plant parents in getting our fortnightly, green-fingered tips." As you get more social proof, as more people join your audience and you get feedback, add it in.

Why not also add in strong reasons why people should sign up. Give them an example of the kinds of emails you send and remind them, "We don't sell your data", or, "You can leave/unsubscribe at any time."

Don't worry about getting a huge number of readers. Focus on getting the *right* people on board, i.e., on improving the quality rather than the quantity. Just remember, everyone starts from zero. I did. You did. The person with the most email subscribers in the world did.

4. Let go (gracefully)

Sometimes people want to go. And you must let them.

Not only is it the correct legal course to take, but blasting emails at your readers and giving them no other option in the hope they'll succumb to Stockholm Syndrome never pans out.

If you use an email platform like MailChimp, they'll automatically handle this for you. But whichever platform you use, it's a good idea to check it is working properly.

Mailbox providers really like the one-click unsubscribe option because it makes life easier for the reader. Making them type out their email address to unsubscribe is annoying because you already know it.

Equally irritating is the, "Email us so we can unsubscribe you", as you never know if this will happen.

And making readers log in is a sure way to get people to click "Mark as Spam", which is so much more damaging than a simple unsubscribe. If lots of people mark your email as spam, it'll be game over for your messages reaching your audience.

Make it as easy as possible for people to leave your list, with a one-click unsubscribe (which is built into most email platforms), and don't forget to test it.

Most platforms will handle the unsubscribe process for you, but it'll look something like:

Manage your emails | Unsubscribe | Trouble viewing?

You are receiving this email because you are a subscriber to Business View. Guardian News & Media Limited - a member of Guardian Media Group PLC. Registered Office: Kings Place, 90 York Way, London, N1 9GU. Registered in England No. 908396

Example 4 – A standard footer with an unsubscribe link.

That's in the footer of an email I don't read anymore, so it's just cluttering up my inbox.

So, I hit Unsubscribe and, as if by magic, it knows who I am and lets me know:

Unsubscribe Confirmation

You have been unsubscribed. These changes can take up to 24 hours to take effect.

Manage your email preferences

Example 5 – Unsubscribe successful.

If you use some home-built systems, or a crazy huge platform, you sometimes end up having to type out your email address again (which is annoying from a reader's point of view) and then still wait up to two weeks to be removed.

The Economist Group

Please confirm the email address you would like to unsubscribe:

E-mail address _____ Unsubscribe

Please note, it may take up to two weeks for you to be unsubscribed from all marketing emails. You may still receive essential service communications from us. View our privacy policy to get more information on how we use your details.

Feedback (optional)

Please let us know the reason why you'd prefer not to receive e-mails from us.

○ You send me too many e-mails   ○ I don't have time to read them
○ They're not relevant to me   ○ Other

Any comments

The Economist Group operates a strict privacy policy around the world.

Example 6 – A painful unsubscribe page.

I've even seen a few sneaky ways to avoid people unsubscribing, such as putting lots of space after an email to make it look like it's ended. (See Example 7 on the next page.)

I'm sure that's an effective way of keeping your subscribers, but I certainly wouldn't advocate it.

Hi Jon,

Have you read the letter I sent out to you yesterday?

It's not very long – but very important *(and quite personal!)*.

It looked like this:

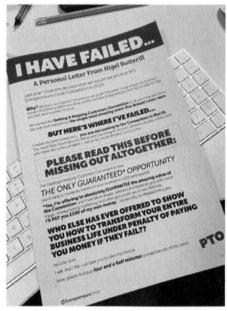

If you haven't read it yet – PLEASE go to: entrepreneurscircle.org/letter ASAP

Any questions let me know!

Nigel

Unsubscribe

Entrepreneurs Circle 2635 Kings Court The Crescent Birmingham B37 7YE United Kingdom 0121 765 5551

Example 7 – Sneaky unsubscribe tactics.

© marketoonist.com

Let people go gracefully!

5. Keep data safe

Since GDPR, people are a lot savvier about how valuable their information is, and the need for it to be protected.

When readers get an email from a brand they don't recognise, they're much more likely to mark it as spam or make a complaint about it, because they know brands should be asking for their consent.

Buying lists in this landscape just doesn't make sense anymore, and there are three main reasons why:

1. You're facing uphill odds of an already low number of people interested enough to make a purchase, coupled with more people willing to opt-out and make complaints.

2. Add in spam honeypot addresses, where fake email addresses
    are hidden on websites so that list-selling businesses
    automatically collect them, and this can wreak havoc on your
    email campaigns.

3. Hostages don't make good customers.

Don't buy a list. Just don't.

6. Build relationships

The best email marketing campaigns are the ones that aren't selling
anything, or at least they don't feel like they are.

Getting a new subscriber is like gaining a new friend. You'll want
to check in on them to make sure your friendship and relationship is
growing. And you want to make it work for them. Nobody wants to sign
up to get offers blasted at them every twenty minutes. (Looking at you,
Groupon!)

How are you adding something useful to the reader's life?

A useful way to think about this is: *"Would I want to receive this email/
sequence?"* Would you want your elderly relative to?

Relationships are two-way, so it's important to be aware of how the
reader can help you (that's normally through making a purchase or
taking action, such as signing a petition or ordering a ticket), but before
asking, always demonstrate how you can help them.

A good general rule of thumb from Gary Vaynerchuk, a social media
expert, in his book *Crushing It!* is, "Jab, jab, jab, right hook", which is a
really American way of saying, "Give, give, give, then ask."

He elaborated in an interview: *"From following people on social, you
know that 99% of people are jerks. Buy my book, buy my wine, come to my
conference, watch this video – it's just push.*

*"Social at its best is you putting out free videos of keynotes and you
answering people's questions and then, on the fifteenth tweet you put out,*

saying, 'Go to Amazon and pre-order my book, that would mean a lot to me.'

"People stop following people that are pushing all the time, or if they don't, they just tune them out.

"We're in a very noisy world. If you don't figure out how to bring value to your reader along the way of you pitching to them, you'll become very irrelevant."

7. Work smarter

Always avoid hard work – try smart work instead, it's a lot less exhausting!

Making things smoother involves getting technical, but it's worth it, as it's about giving the reader a seamless experience.

By trying to get people to buy something they've already bought (unless it's consumable or a regular purchase), you'll be wasting your time and money.

If they've bought one copy of your book, it's unlikely they'll buy another – a bookcase is only so big!

That means making emails relevant and personal, gathering the right information, and getting rid of adverts for purchases they've already made (or changing them to "Buy Again" if it's consumable). This is such an essential function of email platforms that they all offer some way to do this, and I'd 100% recommend starting on this as a quick win.

USING MAILCHIMP: If you're using an email platform like MailChimp, this is relatively straightforward. Just connect up your e-commerce provider, and it will automatically pull in the subscribers' purchase history.

Then, when you create your next campaign, you can select a block and (in MailChimp) go into 'Select Dynamic Content', before setting it to only be shown to people who haven't bought the product you're advertising (if it can be purchased online).

This doesn't work very well with in-person or cash purchases, as they can't be tracked back, but if you're selling things online, it's super easy to do.

> If you use MailChimp, I run a course called Chimp Hero (at chimphero.com), which is all about how to use the features of the world's most popular email platform and make the most of it. MailChimp has some really powerful features that most people miss – so be sure to check it out and learn how it can help your email marketing. If you want to go from MailChump to MailChamp, head to ChimpHero.com. Use coupon BETTEREMAILS for 15% off.

If you've not chosen an email platform, I'd wholeheartedly recommend MailChimp. The last chapter looks more in-depth at how to get set up, and I've included the best competitors so you can pick the one that works for you.

I've got some great examples in Section Three – Chapter 8: *Working Smarter.*

8. Get planning

Emails are like icebergs, as most of the mass (or work) is hidden under the waterline. You'll see other companies, perhaps even competitors' newsletters, but you can't see the work (or lack thereof!) that goes into planning the content out, designing it, getting all the data organised and working out what to send to whom.

Having an overall strategy is excellent, but it's also good to plan out each email as you go, to make sure it's furthering your overall strategy. There's a template for an email brief in Section One – Chapter 2: *Planning Emails.*

Once you've got a strategy together, it's important that everyone in the business has a say and agrees to it. Then make sure you do it and keep it in your mind.

Even if you just stick it on the wall and glance at it every now and again, you'll be seeing it and remembering it.

9. Keep going

Setting expectations upfront is vital. Going to send an email once a month? Once a day? Let prospective readers-to-be know, so they can make an informed choice.

Then stick to it. Honestly, I can be quite terrible at this myself, but don't overpromise. Life can get in the way and it can sometimes feel impossible to send out regularly. Start less frequently and add to it – not the other way round.

Keeping an extra couple of fully created emails can help ease the burden if you're struggling, and, once you get into the rhythm of it and have a bit of a buffer, you'll find it more manageable.

> There are a few templates for you to use and ideas you can adapt in the resources area at sendbetter.email/resources.

Readers will pay attention if you make a promise and then deliver on it and show up. Don't be disheartened if you send out three emails and don't get any immediate sales. Long-term success comes from building up those relationships, and from giving more than asking.

Keep going. You can do it!

10. Send Better Emails

Ask, "How can this email be better?", and write all your ideas down. Every now and again, go through them, make one change and see what happens. Does it make a difference? Now rinse and repeat. Even if you're increasing 1% every month, that's an additional 12% a year you wouldn't otherwise achieve.

Ask your readers how it can be better. Some brands ask people to rate their emails, which is a great way to get quick feedback:

Example 8 – An email feedback example.

Commit right now – go and get your calendar and write it in, review what you're doing and make time for those changes. Incremental little increases soon add up.

As we head into the Email Jigsaw, you can download all the materials, including reader personas and flowcharts, mentioned in this book at sendbetter.email/resources

SECTION ONE – BUILD A STRATEGY

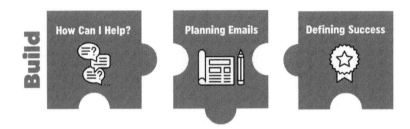

Before we get stuck into the good stuff of recruiting readers and converting them into customers, we need a solid foundation to build on.

If we go in at full speed, 100% promotional, with no benefit for the person reading it, it's not going to get very far.

And if you've no idea of what 'good' looks like, or do not have a target for success, how will you know if it's gone well?

In this section, I'll go through:

- » How can I help? – this is all about adding value to the reader, helping them more than asking them to do something.

- » Planning emails – don't just fire up your email platform and start typing. Create a plan and you'll already be on the path to victory.

- » Defining success – a guide to the business and email metrics you need to know for growth and positive change.

This is a longish section, but stick with me. If you don't get this bit right, there's no real point in doing the rest. Get comfy and get a strong coffee (or a stiff drink!), and let's get started.

Chapter 1: How can I help?

What value can you add to the reader?

If you've ever read a business book, you'll know that the writers of them often bang on about "adding value" for potential customers (who we'll call prospects from now on), and how important that is.

But before I do exactly the same and beat my drum to the same tune, let's take a minute to define what we really mean by adding value, what value is and why we should even consider it, as opposed to the simple batch-and-blast.

Value is a funny word. As a noun, it can mean the worth of something compared to the price paid for it, such as, "That car is being sold for £7k, which is good value." As a verb, it can mean the financial value of an item: "The house is valued at £350k."

In business, and when people talk about "adding value", they mean enhancing the life of your potential customer. That could be through something as simple as making someone chuckle, to curating content (recommending a list of articles and resources from a wide variety of sources) that they might find useful.

In the life of the reader, they get out of bed, have breakfast, take a shower, go to work, come home, make dinner, get back into bed and repeat. Every second is precious.

If they've got children, pets or spouses (or plants!), they've got others relying on them, and there aren't as many free inbox-flicking-through minutes to be had.

The reader checking their emails in those seconds before the kettle boils probably has enough time to quickly clear five emails (maybe more if they live in a hard water area).

A reader's inbox is a precious and coveted space for friends, relatives and brands they like. So, be the brand they love by being part of their life.

"10% OFF NEW STOCK, BUY NOW!" doesn't sound like an email that's going to add anything to their life.

"Choosing the right indoor plants for kids and pets" sounds like a much better email subject line, which would pique the curiosity of our children-having, pet-loving plant parent.

When writing your subject line, think:

→ *Does this add anything to my reader's life?*

→ *Does it make anything easier for them?*

→ *Does it solve a problem they're having?*

→ *Does it make them laugh? (We need more of those!)*

→ *Does it make a positive difference?*

Adding value should underpin that approach of being helpful and putting the readers' interests first.

This is where your strategy comes into play. It's your plan – the physical framework for your approach to adding value. When you plan your content, you can think clearly about what value you're adding to your readers' day. You're not thinking 'on the hop' or going, "Sh*t, I've got to send an email today, what to write?" When you have a strategy, you've got all of this thought out, and it takes the pressure off. Don't underestimate this process. Work smarter, not harder.

Writing this book was quite the task. I had a bit of an idea about what I wanted to talk about and kept going. But it wasn't until I had a strategy that what I had to do became clearer, and thus also a bit easier.

The worst thing you can do is promise something and not deliver it.

For instance, you could have a campaign that says, "Download this free guide on taking care of your plants." This is great, until the reader fills it in, clicks the button and gets either the success page with nothing happening, or a, "Something went wrong" popup, with the reader having no idea why.

In most cases, this is where technology is often to blame. It was set up correctly but hasn't been tested, or the website has been updated, or the tech has broken.

It's almost always not malicious, just that tests are rarely done on automated emails, and any breakages aren't spotted sooner – until clicks and sales start to drop off and the head-scratching begins.

Usually, this is just a case of every month or so signing up with your own email to check it's still working. You'd be surprised how often email service providers like MailChimp update their system without warning that it might break the way their users' websites sign people up.

Don't rely on your subscribers to let you know, they're busy and NOT your email admin!

Help a narrow niche

I hate to sound like every business guru ever, but helping a few people a lot is better than helping loads of people a tiny amount.

Helping people who have quit their corporate job to sell widgets online, because they want to spend more time with their family, is way more specific than just helping 'entrepreneurs'.

By targeting a tiny group of people, you can speak to them in their language – or ideally, if they're like you, you can talk in a shared language. And by language, I don't just mean English, French, German and so on, but the sub-language that people use.

For example, if you're a strategy consultant wanting to speak with CEOs about how you can improve their business, you might be talking about synergy and blue-sky-thinking. In contrast, if you're communicating with younger audiences, it's all about *insert whatever the youth of today are into*.

For our plant company, if we're aiming to reach couples under 40 living in a city flat, we can really target what we say, and we can also really help them. They'll instantly connect with a brand that "helps plant parents brighten up their indoor living space", and there could be tons of relevant content that they feel 'gets them', as opposed to the, "We sell all plants to everyone and here's why you, generic reader, should buy a plant from us", type content.

Give more than you take

Like I said in the Build Relationships commandment, always think about how you jab, jab, jab, hook – or give more than you take.

It's not sleazy to ask for something from your audience. When you build a relationship, it's a two-way street, but when you want to utilise email marketing as an active channel, you're going in for the long game.

You're looking for marriage material with your readers, not just a one-night fling. That might seem counterintuitive for one-off purchases such as a wedding photographer (unless you were Henry VIII's, I guess!). Still, generally, one-time purchases tend to be higher-end or at least more expensive, hence the need for a deeper relationship before you'll commit.

A wedding photographer might have an email sequence that looks like this:

→ Here is a list of shots everyone should have at their wedding.

→ Read this bank of questions you should ask when you interview/choose your photographer.

→ How to organise group photographs with step-relatives that can't stand each other.

You'd be left thinking: *That photographer really knows what they're on about. And the free advice is great.* If you're looking to supercharge your emails, try to handle any objections (like pricing or how payment works) as part of it, with the primary aim to land more clients.

Chapter 2: Planning emails

Reader persona

You might already have a customer persona, perhaps several, and this is a great place to start when it comes to developing your reader persona, although the latter is a bit different. (Don't worry if you haven't got any personas, there's a template coming up.)

A persona is a semi-fictional character that typifies your target customer. You might have one, a few, or several. It's helpful to visualise them, as this expresses the variety of customers you have.

It's best to attach a name to them and really picture who they are. If you don't have any customers at the moment, this will be a bit more difficult, but if you're already trading, pick a few averages. For example, if you have customers who all fit into the same age range, and have the same types of jobs and needs, this would be a great persona.

When I started Inbox Hero, my first few customers were called Helen. They were around about the same age, and I focused on making all my marketing materials predominantly speak to this persona. It really helped me to understand the problems that the Helens of the world were facing, and I could talk directly to them about how I could help.

Our example plant store is aimed at younger people who live in flats. I'm going to call our persona Jess. She's 25, not currently in a relationship and is enjoying being young and living in a city (read: likes partying and Tuesday tequilas). She earned a degree a few years ago but is still close with her university friends. She's outgoing socially, as well as ambitious and driven professionally. Jess really wants a pet but rents her flat, so a plant is the next best thing. She wants some help getting the right indoor plants for her space, and to learn how to keep them alive.

Your persona should be specific enough that there are at least a few customers who might vaguely match this description, but not so precise that it only applies to one person on earth. Think along the lines of, if everyone curtsies to them, calls them ma'am as in ham, rather than ma'am as in farm, and they love corgis.

To get your persona down pat, you could add in further supplemental information, e.g., Jess is a brunette, wears glasses, is recovering from a bad breakup and *add stereotypical young adult things in here*. This last bit will just help you to visualise them, but be careful how far you take it. You don't suddenly want to start talking about how this plant is the best for brunettes – that just sounds creepy!

Your reader persona should cover all the people who read your emails, despite the fact some of them will never make a purchase.

Customer personas look at who buys, but they're also essential in identifying who doesn't buy, and why that's the case. It might be that Jess prefers to shop online and that the plant shop doesn't offer e-commerce or postage, so there's no way for a relationship to bloom.

If you don't already have a customer persona, check out hubspot.com/make-my-persona.

There are several questions you can ask to really draw out the detail of your reader persona, and having it planned out, with a clear idea of who your reader is, will really help you in the later chapters.

Once you've established your reader persona(s), you can better speak to their hopes, dreams and fears, rather than trying to grab everyone with a small fishing net.

You can download the one-page sheet over the page from sendbetter.email/resources. I recommend printing and sketching out as many as you feel represent your audience.

Reader Persona

Who is your reader?	What else are they doing just before/after reading your emails?	Where do they read your emails?	How long have they got when they read your emails?	Demographics

What other emails do they receive?	

Why do/did they sign up? (The need)	What value do your emails add? (The solution)

When (day and time) is best for them to read your emails?	What device are they reading your email on?

Who isn't your reader? (Who do you want to repel from signing up)

An example Reader Persona template that you can download and fill in.

Here are some 'Starter for Ten' questions to ponder:

→ *Who are your readers?*

A good place to start is with some of your current subscribers. So, do a bit of cyber-sleuthing and become a digital Sherlock Holmes.

If they've got a business email address, where do they work?

If they've purchased something from you, where do they live? (Which city or country is useful; a GPS coordinate is probably a bit much.)

If they open your emails, when do they tend to open them? Most email platforms will let you delve into a contact's history, and you can build a bit of a picture of your reader. If they've opened your last five emails at 3am, they might be a night owl, or they might have a newborn.

You don't need to do this for everyone, or in great depth – the idea is to find some common trends.

And you never know, it might bring out some useful information that will help you focus your business outside of emails, too.

→ *How can you find out more about them?*

This one is quite easy – ask them!

Run a survey (SurveyMonkey offer a free version), with some basic questions about why they signed up, etc., so you can understand them better.

Reader feedback is extremely valuable. I always ask them to let me know what they're finding useful or to suggest improvements, and you can get some great insights. (This ties in nicely with my Send Better Emails Commandment, too!)

→ *How can you find out more about new subscribers as they sign up?*

Again – ask them. You might have a sign-up form that asks the reader for their name, email address and a question about the biggest problem they're facing right now that you can solve.

For example, if the owners of Poppy's Plants suddenly started seeing loads of new sign ups who said they lived in houses with gardens, that might prompt them to stock more outdoor plants – or to promote different products in their newsletter.

So, you've got a good basic grasp of your readers. That's excellent. Repeat that exercise every year or so to make sure you're still relevant, but also so you can stay that way.

Want to take it to the next level? These questions can be really useful:

→ *Where do they read your emails?*

→ *How long have they got when they read your emails?*

→ *What other emails do they receive or are signed up to?*

→ *When (day of the week and time) is best for them to read your emails?*

So, using our persona of Jess, let's look at how she starts her journey.

The path to fandom

There are mainly 3 reasons why Jess will sign up:

1. **To get a free download.**
2. **To get an immediate discount.**
3. **Because they want to (no reward or incentive).**

There's nothing wrong with incentivising prospective readers with a discount or download to get them to sign up, it's how you'll often see it done on other websites, and it's a great way to grow your list.

But to really grow it, you should consider using more than one approach (if you're not already).

It's also a great way to get people to take their first step on the path to fandom. In the business world, you'll find it called the *Ladder of Customer Loyalty*, and it proposes that everyone you meet falls into one of five rungs on the ladder:

1. Suspects

   At the bottom are suspects. They don't really know very much about you. They've come across your company and are aware of you, but that's it. Everyone starts here.

2. Prospects

   Once they're interested in what you've got to offer, they're climbing the ladder. Now, your reader is a prospect, and this is where emails (and other marketing channels) can help them to climb further.

3. Customers

They were interested in what you had to sell, liked what they saw and bought it. If it goes well, they might come back.

4. Clients

They loved it, they're back for more, and they're really vibing when it comes to your relationship. This is typically where most marketing ends, but the ultimate path to fandom has one more rung . . .

5. Advocates/superfans

They're so happy with your product or service that they buy again and again, and tell others about you. They're incredibly valuable, and the best email marketing programmes can keep them happy with loyalty rewards, discounts and special events.

Some brands even give them a nickname or have a 'VIP club'.

The aim of email marketing (and marketing in general) is to push suspects up to prospects and convince prospects to jump up to customers. It can help with (alongside great products and services) moving them up to clients and, hopefully, superfans. Not everyone will get there, but that shouldn't stop you trying.

There are a few pros and cons to the following approaches to growing your list:

1. To get a free download

You might hear this being called 'lead generation'. It's the idea that you give something away for free in exchange for someone's email address.

This is a great way to demonstrate that you know what you're talking about, but I always highlight the need to ensure that the download is top-notch, as it'll be one of the first impressions potential customers will get of you.

Don't give away free sh*t – give away free gold.

I always recommend letting people know that they'll get added to the list (and for brownie points, with a link to an example mailing, so they'll know what they're getting into) and being clear they can unsubscribe at any time.

When Jess enters her email address, ensure that the first email she receives has the free download she originally asked for and highlight that she can expect to get emails every week/fortnight/month.

I'd also suggest pointing out that she can unsubscribe at any time. So, if she didn't want to get anymore emails (which readers are entirely allowed to do!), Jess could quickly hit the unsubscribe button.

2.   To get an immediate discount

This can be an excellent way to push wavering customers over the line to make a purchase, and from experience, it definitely works.

It's often a popup on a website offering a discount code in the checkout for signing up. Alternatively, sometimes readers sign up to a form that might say, for example, "Get exclusive offers and deals."

The drawback is that you can sometimes 'cannibalise' your own revenue. That's to say that some of those people might have made a purchase anyway, maybe even at the retail price or a lower discount price, meaning you would have made more profit.

A wool shop I worked with gave its subscribers a 10% discount, thinking it would boost sales a little. Sales went up, but it was more successful than anticipated, to the point where it was hurting profit too much, and the offer had to be withdrawn.

If given a nudge that there were new colours in stock, some of those subscribers may well have purchased their wool at the full price. The easiest way to know is to test it.

Run a discount for a month and then withdraw it for a month, and see what happens.

Always experiment – even with the discount level.

Another business I worked with has a regular sale. It puts bums on seats, as everyone loves a bargain, but if the discount was lower, or even not there at all, would some of those people have bought anyway?

Further experiments showed that for that particular business, the 'goldilocks' balance between the number of sales and profitability was 35% off.

That won't be the same for you, so try experimenting for one month doing one thing, and the next trying something else. Later, you can compare the results to see what's working well (and drop what's not).

3. Just because they want to

This takes a bit more work to promote. You might let your social media followers know you're about to send out another newsletter and they need to sign up by 5pm to get it – or you could put it in your email signature (a fantastic, free advertising slot!).

The best way to promote signing up without an incentive is by giving convincing reasons for why readers should do so – and that's why the reader persona exercise is useful in helping you to talk to your readers in their own dialect.

This means you've really got to sell it. "Sign up to get my emails" is a typical call-to-action, but it doesn't tell potential readers what to expect or, most importantly, why they should sign up.

"Sign up to our Plant Parent newsletter and get all the best tips to keep your little ones green and happy" is an example of how to be clear, and it's a good way to grow a list without that dangling carrot.

I always suggest creating a version of this so you can promote the value of your newsletter outside of your website, or attract readers that aren't yet ready enough to purchase.

After I've sent out 'Emails Explained' (my fortnightly email marketing newsletter, it's very meta), I post a link to the email (all providers will give you a link you can use to share a web version of the email) to my LinkedIn social media profile, with what it's about and how you can subscribe.

I always get new subscribers. People can see the quality of the newsletter, and by dropping hints that only your subscribers get the golden tips, it builds a fear of missing out.

When I went public that I was writing this book, the first people I told were my subscribers. I later posted on social media, but I bragged, "My subscribers heard about this last week", to drive even more potential readers to sign up.

Here are a few ideas on different ways you could promote your list:

- » Tell your followers on social media why they should sign up.
- » Drop it into the conversation at networking meetings.
- » Add it into your email signature.
- » Add it as a call-to-action on blog posts.
- » Reference it in your YouTube videos.
- » Every time a newsletter goes out, post a web link to it on social media to try and recruit social media followers to your list of email subscribers.
- » At the end of a call with a prospective client.

The one-page email brief

For significant emails, such as product launches or critical holidays, you might want to think about creating a plan for that email.

Planning it out can give your email more purpose, and setting a goal (such as revenue or number of sales) can really shift your decision-making skills up a gear.

A full, two-page download of an email brief template is available at sendbetter.email/resources, but have a think about the last few emails you've sent, or the ones you are planning to send.

Now, think about how answering the following questions might boost the focus of your email. Not all the questions will be relevant, and some of them might not be suitable for you, but have a think:

→ *WHO should get this message?*

- All subscribers?

- A particular segment?

- Only those taking an action? (Such as abandoning a checkout basket.)

→ *WHAT action do you want those subscribers to take?*

- Make a purchase or donation?

- Register for an event?

- Use a hashtag on social media?

→ *WHY will those subscribers be motivated to take that action?*

- A discount?

- A deadline?

- Compelling information?

- Emotional appeal?

→ *WHEN should those subscribers receive the message?*

- Immediately?

- On a certain day?

- In the morning, afternoon or evening?

→ *HOW will you measure this email's success?*

- Revenue?
- Downloads?
- Leads?
- Clicks?
- Opens?

→ *IS this email part of a series of messages or a subscriber or customer journey?*

- How does this email build on previous ones and set up the next?

→ *DO you have any supplementary material that's important to answering any of the previous questions?*

- Case study?
- Blog post?
- Competitor's email?

Now, go into your inbox and look at the last ten promotional emails you've received. This could be your work email, but you'll probably find better marketing emails in your personal inbox.

How do you think those companies might have answered those questions?

This reverse engineering can really bring to the fore the desperation that can sometimes come through on over salesy emails, and it can also give you some inspiration on what gels with you and what you really don't like.

Planning is the cornerstone for success in anything, and email marketing is no exception.

The automation sequences every business needs

Automated email sequences are emails that go out to customers, normally because they've done something . . . made a purchase, downloaded an eBook or signed up to your email list. These happen automatically, and while it requires a bit of effort upfront, it's then just a case of light maintenance to check they're all up to date every now and again.

Most email platforms call them 'Automations' or 'Triggered' email campaigns, but before you log in and play around with a new tool, I want to talk about the importance of planning it out (strategy) before trying to build it (tactic).

Lots of platforms will dazzle you with a huge number of examples and templates, and it can be hard to know where to start. Others give you a blank slate and tell you to get on with it. I always recommend thinking about what automated email sequences you might want to implement, drawing them out like a flowchart, with a little summary about each email, and then building them.

> » First up is the **welcome sequence**. If you do nothing else, get one of these. This will normally make up the first few interactions a reader will have with you, so it's super important to get it right. It's so important I've got a whole chapter called *Saying Hello*, so feel free to stick around for that one, or nip over there, read it through and then come back.

> » Next up is the **post-purchase sequence**, for businesses that take payments online. This crucial step is often neglected. The chapter *What's Next?* covers how to think through the post-purchase sequence.

> » Most online shops have the ability to send **abandoned basket emails**, and these can convert those readers sitting on the fence. This is money left on the table, as these readers got to the checkout but didn't get around to buying – for whatever reason. An automated reminder that they left something behind,

commonly sent with a discount code, can be enough to convert more than a few readers into customers.

» For those looking for a challenge, there's the **win-back sequence.** This is where if a reader doesn't open any emails for a while, you try to re-engage them and warm them back up to their former glory of waiting with bated breath for your every word (or email, I suppose!). If you're keen to give this a go, I've got a more detailed write up in *Why Data Is King.*

Download the flowcharts for these automations at
sendbetter.email/resources

Deciding which automation sequences will suit you best can be daunting, and if after reading this you're still unsure how to nail down the ones that will be your best fit, let's get a Power Hour booked in and have a chat. Have a look at my calendar at sendbetter.email/powerhour

Chapter 3: Defining success

Action-based planning

The goal of emails should be to make the reader *take action*.

That action might be making a purchase, signing a petition or registering for an event ticket.

Have that action as the clear goal in your mind. Forget about open rates (for the minute!), let's focus on action.

Let's send out a newsletter to our 1,000 plant shop subscribers. Here's a few ideas of good content to include:

» A short write up about something recent – it's almost always weather-related!

» Get 30% off in the succulent Saturday sale!

» A couple of featured succulents with a Buy Now option.

» An article about plant care.

» A video from YouTube about a funny plant.

» A friendly 'have a good week' note.

» A plug of National Indoor Plant Week (you can always find something at nationaldaycalendar.com).

Now, the reader could take action in several ways. They could click Buy Now, or they could read the article or watch the video. There are some social media links in the footer, so the reader might also click on those.

It's important that the goal is clear and fairly near the top, so the readers who don't scroll all the way to the bottom will still see it.

On a very long email, it's also an idea to consider repeating the button (or copying the button and using different text). This is especially important on mobiles, where the format is portrait and users can scroll faster than on desktops. You might have a button at the top directing readers to the sale and also near the bottom.

Readers tend to only scroll in one direction – downwards. So, if there's a really important action they should take, repeat it later on.

I worked with a marketing manager once who swore blind that emails should be stuffed with links, because then readers will click something, anything.

That's kind of true. More chances to click tends to result in more overall clicks, but if you've got twenty different videos, articles and offers pulling readers in all directions, it can become confusing.

Beware of asking the reader to do too many actions. Once a reader has clicked on a link, they're unlikely to come back to the email with the same focus and pick up where they left off.

Be clear. Try to only have one main action.

We could group different types of actions into two camps.

1. First, there are *powerful actions*, like making a purchase or signing a petition. Let's call these **Primary Actions**. They're what you really want people to do.

2. Then there are actions that are *useful*, such as reading a blog post or watching a video. These could contain calls to make a purchase, but just the act of reading isn't a Primary Action. So, let's call these **Secondary Actions**. They're useful, but the main aim of these should be to point back to a Primary Action.

Let's have a look at a few examples:

Primary Actions	Secondary Actions
	All of these are secondary, unless they have a Primary Action in mind, like 'read an article that has a coupon code for a sale'.
→ Make a purchase	→ Read an article
→ Sign a petition	→ Learn more
→ Register for an event	→ Visit a website (if not with a Primary Action in mind)
→ Sign up for a free trial	→ Watch a video
→ Renew your account	
→ Upgrade your plan	
→ Recommend a friend	
→ Sign up to volunteer	
→ Log in to change your account	
→ Vote in an election	

Be careful not to mistake readers' clicking (or ending up where that click lands) with an action taken. As we'll get to in a minute, the funnel for email metrics involves opens, clicks and actions. A click isn't the final destination, the action is.

You'll see in the table that I've put reading articles as a **Secondary Action**. Often, clients will ask me, "Why is that?"

Knowing something (*passively* reading or watching a video about it) and doing something (*taking action*) are two polarly opposed forces.

I know I need to get into shape, but exercise is hard work. I know I should go to a gym, but buying a membership, putting on my kit and heading out at 6am in the dark takes a lot more effort than simply 'knowing' I ought to.

REAL-WORLD EXAMPLE

In 2012, the world was ablaze with hatred for African dictator Joseph Kony, after a documentary came out exposing the Ugandan cult and militia leader.

Millions signed up on Facebook to march against this injustice. They shared information via social media, which at this point was still in its relative infancy, and helped to get the message out far and wide.

Almost everyone connected to the internet or who had access to a newspaper knew about the horrendous war crimes Kony was accused of.

And then when it came to taking action, for people to gather, march on their governments and petition the people in power?

Nothing.

But it generated a heck of a lot of donations for the charity that made the documentary, so maybe that's the real action at work!

Getting readers to take the desired action isn't as tricky as it sounds. Just:

» Be clear about what you want.

» Make your buttons stand out.

» Use active language.

» Be immediate.

I'll go into these points in more detail throughout this chapter, but it's important here to understand how we can be clear about the action we want people to take, so we can visualise it and plan it.

Be clear about what you want

Don't beat around the bush. If you want to convert readers into customers, avoiding the words *Buy Now* might confuse them. You might miss out on people who are interested in making a purchase.

If it's a product-focused email, *Buy Now, Shop Now* and *Get Yours Now* are all perfectly legitimate calls-to-action. Try to keep it to no more than three words, otherwise it might not be snappy enough.

It's even better if you make it clear what you want people to do while making it fit your brand voice. A good example for a jewellery store enticing brides to find their ring might be: *Discover your style*. It's clear that at this stage you're still looking. Even better, in this situation, the bride will want to find the perfect ring without price considerations. After all, the groom is the one that will pony up.

Read More is a well-used way to tease an article in a newsletter and then push the reader onto a website. It works because it's crystal clear. You could try to be a little more creative with: *Explore More* or *Get Started*, or you could use whatever the article is about, such as *Learn About*.

Make buttons great again

Buttons are great. You can use them to communicate different things. Big buttons for important CLICK ME actions to be taken, and smaller buttons for less important actions or information.

Buttons should be big, clear and loud. It should be immediately obvious it is a button, and also where that button is going to take you.

If possible, being on-brand colour wise is good, but making sure your button stands out is key. Many users simply skim or glance at emails, so bright and eye-catching buttons can help arrest the mindless scroll.

In the button game, size really does matter. Informally, I've run quite a few tests on this, and this was the case for all the brands I experimented on. It does kind of make sense. Bigger button = clearer action to be taken.

As Alex Heath, Chief Customer and Marketing Officer at RAC said in the foreword: *"Whether building and nurturing your email list, driving consumer engagement or converting to sales – it's all about incremental, and often marginal, gains."*

Bigger buttons

An increase in button size and button text size saw a few more clicks than the regular-sized button. It's not going to be at the top of your to-do list, but testing what buttons to use, the text and how big they are might yield some interesting results for you – and help you identify where you can squeeze out tiny improvements later down the line.

Example 9 – Larger buttons can increase clicks, especially on a mobile.

It might sound silly, but fat-fingered mobile users will be thankful.

Use active language

When I talk about writing actively, I mean snappy, short, action-based words or sentences. Let's get people pumped up for action! We're likely to find a verb (or doing word) here, too, probably along the lines of *Buy, Subscribe, Shop, Explore, Discover.*

In technical terms, an active voice is when the subject (main focus) of a sentence performs the verb's action. An example would be **monkeys adore bananas.**

→ Monkeys are the **subject** here, *doing* the **action** of adoring.

→ Adore is the **action.**

→ And bananas are yummy and, in this case, the **object.**

But if you flip it around and a passive voice is used, this is where the subject is acted on by the verb. The example would be **bananas are adored by monkeys.**

→ Bananas here are still yummy and the **object.**

→ Adore is still the **action.**

→ Monkeys are the **subject,** but the **action** is happening *to* them, and they're not doing anything.

Back in our email marketing, this might be expressed as:

→ **Active:** If you have any questions, call me on 0117 369 0030.

→ **Passive:** If there are any questions, I can be reached at the number below.

You can see the active is communicating the same thing, just in a punchier way. That 'call me' action is an obvious thing to do, much more so than 'being reached out to'.

Be immediate

Buy Now works because of two words:

→ *Buy* – this is the **action** you want the reader to take.

→ *Now* – this is *when* you want the reader to complete that **action**.

I ran a large test of this using two different button texts:

→ *Get Cover* – pretty straightforward. You want cover? Get it.

→ *Get Cover Now* – the same, but more.

That extra word made the button slightly longer, but it improved the click rate by a couple of percentage points – proving the hypothesis, in this case, that the immediacy element can be a useful tool to further spur readers into *action*.

Imagine seeing these buttons:

→ '*Buy Sometime Next Week*' or '*Shop Whenever*'!

Having a goal that has a clear line on the **action** to take will help you on the path to success. Speaking of this, how should we measure it?

The business metrics for success

The question of what success is can be tricky to wrestle with. If you know what your goal is (sales) then shouldn't measuring it be easy and involve simply checking the cash register?

In a disappointing retort, yes and no.

Open rates don't, by themselves, dictate the cash in the register, so it's useful to have a look at a few things that do.

Welcome to business basics 101! Today, we'll be learning about the different numbers that determine your bottom line, and how you can improve each of them.

There's no need for a calculator, as this is just theory, but it might be an idea to sit down afterwards to try and work them out for your business, before sketching out some ideas on how they can be improved.

A few templates and examples you might find useful to print out and work through are available at sendbetter.email/resources, and there are some blog posts and resources all about the metrics for success for email marketing at sendbetter.email/metrics.

If you're curious and want to dive deeper, for example, by looking into how to measure coupon usage, redemption rates and price waterfalling, I recommend the book *Marketing Metrics: The Definitive Guide to Measuring Marketing Performance* by Neil T. Bendle, Paul W. Ferris and David J. Reibstein. I used this for my university degree in marketing, and it's ideal for those looking to explore further.

Average Order Value

What it is: *The average value (in local currency) that an order is equal to (minus delivery and service fees).*

Example:

→ You have one customer that has spent £100 on each of their three orders.

→ Another customer that has spent £150 on one order and £50 on another.

→ And another who has spent £10 on each of their five orders.

→ Averaging this out, this would be first customer {£100 + £100 + £100} + second customer {£150 + £50} + third customer {£10 x five} = £550 from 10 orders, making the **average order value = £55.**

How to improve it:

→ **Cross sell** – this is offering related products to the one being looked at (think of offering a bottle of orchid feed when someone buys an orchid).

→ **Upsell** – this is offering a larger or more expensive version of the product (think of a bigger version of the same plant, or a bigger pot that has more flowers in it).

→ **Volume discount** – this is offering a discount if you buy over a certain quantity.

→ **Free shipping** for a higher minimum purchase.

→ **Coupons** – one could offer 10% off purchases over £50, to increase the minimum purchase.

→ **Donations** to a charity for a higher minimum purchase.

→ A better **return policy** for higher priced items.

Customer Lifetime Value

What it is: *The average of the total value of ALL orders from a customer.*

Example:

→ You have one customer that has spent £100 on three orders (totalling £300).

→ Another customer that has spent £150 on one order and £50 on another (totalling £200).

→ And another who has spent £10 on ten orders (totalling £100).

→ Averaging this out, this would be £200 (£300+£200+£100 = £600/3 customers = £200 per customer).

How to improve it:

→ Increase the amount of each order.

→ Increase the number of orders.

→ Decrease life expectancy of order consumables – this is where you might sell something that lasts a year, but you might then choose to sell a cheaper, smaller version that needs replacing more often.

→ Increase how long customers stay loyal to you.

→ Decrease any Churn Rate (explained below).

Churn Rate

What it is: *For membership organisations, this is how many people (as a %) cancel their membership every time it's billed.* The term is also used for products with a contract, such as insurance or broadband.

Example:

→ You have 1,000 members and they pay monthly. If 10 members leave every month, that's 1,000/10 = 1% churn rate. Membership companies are on the hunt to reduce this by any means necessary.

How to improve it:

→ Increase engagement with members throughout the lifetime of their membership.

→ Give clear lines of communication for when they experience problems.

→ Decrease the ease of cancelling – this is normally done through not having an online cancellation feature and having customers phone in and speak to someone, where you might be able to offer a discount or an incentive to stay.

The ultimate measure of success for all your marketing should be aligned to how you do business. There are several business models, but to simplify things, let's look at three.

1. **Poppy's Plants** – The classic retail model.

   You could buy one or several plants now, and at any point in the future.

   The best measurements of success would be Average Order Value and Customer Lifetime Value.

2. **Poppy's Plants by Post** – The membership model.

   You buy one membership and pay the same amount every month or year.

   The best measurement of success would be Customer Lifetime Value and Churn Rate.

3. **Poppy's Exotic Plants and Trees** – The high-ticket retail model.

   You'll buy one, it'll cost a lot and you'll be unlikely to buy another soon.

   The best measurement of success would be Average Order Value and Total Number of Orders.

Depending on the business model, the way to increase overall revenue doesn't always mean more sales.

Let that sink in for a minute.

More revenue doesn't have to mean recruiting more customers.

Increasing the average order value, the number of purchases and reducing the churn rate are all great ways for different business types to make more money from the same number of people.

We will be talking later about building your list, but it's important not to blindly focus on growing (working hard) when you could be looking at defining and optimising success (working smart).

Now that we've covered the business basics for measuring success, let's take a look at how this comes into play with email marketing.

Email metrics

Almost every day, I see or get asked the question: "What's a good open rate?", and my answer never changes: "It depends."

It depends on a lot of things, but usually it's **around 20%.**

"20%?" I hear from the back. "I've got 90% – I must be doing amazingly!"

Yes, you are. That's a great start. But that's why it depends. If you've only got people on your list who you know personally, then all those people will engage with you. Because they know and (hopefully!) like you.

Once you get to second-degree connections, that number is likely to drop and hang around 40%. Then, when you're sending to mostly the general public, people you've not personally spoken with (or third-degree plus connections), the baseline standard is 20%.

But herein lies the dilemma – is the open rate the best goal for your email campaign?

If you're trying to get readers to buy something, it doesn't matter if your open rate is 9% or 99%, because in itself that doesn't generate sales.

Whatever action you're trying to get the reader to perform, it always boils down to pushing people down the 'email funnel' of open, click, action. In our plant shop example that action is sales.

It's perfectly normal to lose people at every stage.

Take a look at the email funnel example on the next page.

Example 10 – The email engagement funnel.

We're sending a newsletter out with some plant care tips and some new varieties of succulent that have just come in. We want to get some sales, but to accurately estimate a sales target, we need to have a look at all the things readers have to do to get there.

Let's do some basic maths! *It'll be over quickly, I promise.*

Say we've got 1,000 subscribers and a weekend sale on.

» A 20% open rate means 200 people open and read the newsletter.

» 20% of those who open click through to the site – that's 40 people.

» 20% of those get through the process of picking a plant and placing their order, meaning 8 new orders. (These are conversions, or the action we're hoping people take.)

From 1,000 subscribers we've got 8 new orders. That might not seem like a lot, but that's pretty standard when you get to expanding your email list to people you don't directly know. (And could you really know a thousand people very well?)

How often will you measure/track them?

The big question when getting started with measuring success with email marketing is: *how do you track it?*

For e-commerce, this can be really simple. Your email platform (MailChimp) will automatically add tags onto every link in your email. Your website or e-commerce provider will see this, and you should be able to view the total number of people that came to your site and then made a purchase.

Normally, this is through a tool like Google Analytics, which is free and very easy to set up.

It's important to set it up so you can measure what's making an impact. For example, if you sent out an email and posted on social media about your new range of succulents, and then all of a sudden there was a huge surge in demand, how would you know where that demand came from?

MailChimp can connect directly into your website and you can view your sales data on its dashboard, too. That's why I always recommend it as a great platform for those getting started. You can learn more about the integrations in my Chimp Hero course at chimphero.com

Against what time period will you compare?

It's important to regularly measure your email marketing metrics, like the open and click rates. For most people, this will be once a week or once a fortnight. Try to make sure it's done regularly and maybe even add a recurring event in your calendar to do it, as if there's a problem, you won't see it until you've lost some sales.

Unless you're a huge company, don't worry about doing it every day. You'll always see slight differences depending on the time of day and the day of the week. Do it regularly, but don't obsess over it.

How can I increase success?

Don't just focus on improving the number.

Success is more than just improving metrics. (Although that is a large part of it!)

When you send an email, you can compare it to other emails you've sent in the past. You can then use that knowledge to work out whether it performed better or worse, and why that might be.

It's this type of learning, which involves trying to figure out the causes of performance going up or down, that is key to improving your emails to bring you future success.

Open rates

What is the open rate made up of and how does it work?

The open rate is controlled by three things:

1. From name

2. Subject line

3. Preview text

As I said earlier, when I talked about the 'email funnel', this is the first step where people fall off, so making sure that all three are as good as they can be will help to increase the open rate.

How to increase open rates

From name

You'll always hear that the most important things for boosting open rates are the subject line and the preview text. But that's not entirely true. It also relies on the from name.

This is often overlooked, but it can be tweaked to improve engagement.

Let's have a look at how Poppy's Plants might do a late January push for St. Valentine's Day:

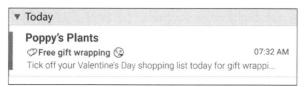

We can clearly see the from name at the top. It's the biggest text size of all the lines and it has the most prominence, so it's worth spending a bit of time thinking about it.

Some companies prefer to send as themselves, or a mixture, such as "Jon from Inbox Hero."

This from name is very short. Longer subject lines and even longer preview texts will draw the reader's eyes down. It's not the only way to do it, but if you check your inbox, you'll see that most email marketing naturally defaults to this.

But if you've got a big sale on or want to cram in a couple more words, why not see if the from name could give you a little leg up?

We've got the scream-in-your face "It's an offer!" option:

Or there's a way to try and sneak in a bit of seasonality:

Or make it personal and local:

REAL-WORLD RESULT

I worked on some 'from name testing' with a client, and the results were interesting.

It was a test to see whether adding "–Half price sale" to the end of the from name made any difference.

It increased the open rate by just under 4%. But what happened later down the email funnel was that clicks rose by 24% and revenue was up 49% against the version that just had the company name.

While it only pushed a few more people to open the email, those extra readers had a much higher 'purchase intent' (meaning they were much more likely to complete the checkout and end up making a purchase).

It was a phenomenal result that snowballed at every step in the funnel.

Subject lines

Subject lines are what most people will think about when they're trying to improve open rates.

There are five key ways to improve your subject lines:

1. Talk to the reader

Like I've harped on about in Section One – Chapter 1: *How Can I Help?*, the easiest way to develop long-term email marketing results is to be helpful. Subject lines can use this by talking *to* the reader, rather than at them.

If we think about how we can make promotional emails talk more to the reader, we have to think about what they might want and how we can help them. I remember talking to a business coach once about focusing on customer benefits. He said, "People don't buy drills because they want a drill. People buy drills because what they really want is the result. They're buying the hole in the wall, not the drill."

Working this through to our subject line, instead of "50% off our drills", try, "Half price holes in your wall." The latter speaks to the customer in a way the former doesn't. And it stands out a little.

2. Excitement

Subject lines help readers to go, "Hmmm, should I open that email in the finite time I have to check my inbox?", so it's disappointing to see so many senders not capitalising on it. BE EXCITING! You have to stand out.

Now, not every business can get away with being as edgy as BrewDog or as sweary as Billy Connolly, and I get it – if you're a funeral director it's a bit limiting (unless you put the fun in funeral!), but wheel out a pun or two on occasion and see how your audience reacts.

The crime most email campaigns are guilty of – and I'm sometimes not entirely innocent of this myself – is spending way too much time on the content of the email and not enough on the subject line. And as we learned earlier, if people don't open the email, they can't see the great images, copy and buttons to click on.

Use pop culture references, different capitalisation or interesting punctuation (square brackets, anyone?), anything to stand out from the millions of other emails being sent at the same time.

3. Urgency

Used appropriately, urgency and making reminders stand out can have a really big impact on open rates.

I oversaw an A/B test for two similar subject lines:

» "Don't forget to book your appointment."

» "REMINDER: Don't forget to book your appointment."

That extra "REMINDER:" doubled the open rate. Sometimes, the best thing to do is keep it simple, and by just making the reminder stand out you can improve performance.

A word of caution, though, don't use it unnecessarily. I've seen some [ACTION REQUIRED] prefixes to marketing emails that absolutely didn't require action – that's the kind of thing that will push readers to angrily unsubscribe, or worse, report as spam. So, don't overdo it.

4. Brevity

Subject lines aren't all about trying to cram in as much information as possible. They tend to get cut off on mobile phones anyway. Why not try making a really short one? That'll stand out against a wall of text.

There's a scene in the film *Hot Fuzz*, when the new cop in town is out for a jog and a strange man runs up alongside him (it later transpires he's the local supermarket manager) and declares, "I'm a slasher and I must be stopped. A slasher . . . of prices!" A bit of a creepy introduction perhaps, but let's see how that unique interaction could be played out as a marketing email.

To:	St Nicholas Angel
From:	Simon Skinner
Subject line:	Slasher
Preview text:	I must be stopped
Email Text:	Lock me up.
	I'm a slasher.
	A slasher . . . of prices.
	These discounts are criminal.
	Buy now >

The whole email, including the from name, subject line, preview text and body copy, is 23 words. It's certainly striking – although a little bit chilling!

5. Just a smidge of clickbait

Being specific about how you can help can go a long way.

These are some great examples from OptinMonster:

» "Grow your email list 10X ⚡ faster with these 30 content upgrade ideas."
» "✔ 63-Point Checklist for Creating the Ultimate Optin Form."
» "212 blog post ideas."

They're all helpful, but they've all got just a little clickbait to them. Not too much.

Too much tends to be found in political campaign fundraising emails (and I've got some terrible examples coming up!)

POWER UP

A/B testing

The best way to use subject lines is to do some A/B tests. Every email platform will give you this ability, which involves sending out two identical versions of the email, but with different subject lines. Repeat this a few times and you'll start to build a picture of what works.

Don't take the tired statistic that "emojis improve open rates by over 55%!", because it's not true – or rather, it's not true for everyone. You'd think this would work. After all, emojis add colour to the subject line and all the cool kids love them, right? For two businesses I've worked with that have demographically older readers, the reverse was true and emojis actually hurt the open rate. Others that have younger audiences saw some a bit higher, but most remained predominantly flat.

Every business has its own unique audience, so it's important to think about experimenting and testing on yours, before building your own "this works for my readers" ideas.

There are a few examples of how not to do it. If you use Twitter, look up the #DarkPatternsOfEmail from Dylan Smith, who has highlighted the latest shady practices and is continuously adding to them.

Here are a few examples that will make you a little queasy.

» Pretending a marketing email is a support ticket:

MealPal	12:05 >
Re: [Ticket #:1987356] 40% off	
Update on your 40% off request View this email in your browser...	

Example 11 – Marketing email disguised as a customer-service reply

» Pretending a campaign donation email is an order receipt:

Subject line: "Your Order #202045 – One hour to CONFIRM"

» Pretending a campaign donation email is a survey:

Subject line: "🖊 Your Post-Election Survey"

» Masquerading an abandoned basket email (an email sent when a reader adds a product to their basket but doesn't complete the purchase) as a purchase receipt:

Subject line: "Your order #29471 has been confirmed. Free shipping was applied."

» Changing the From/Sender Name to make it look like a thread:

From name: "me, Joe (2)"

» Deliberately making the opt-out form confusing, so it's not clear whether you're actually opting out:

In the following example, if you click Yes, it actually subscribes you. It's weird.

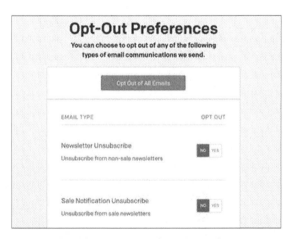

Example 12 – A very confusing opt-out form.

© marketoonist.com

I love this cartoon, because it totally encapsulates what happens when we obsess over the open rate.

Sure, you can make it spike, but that's not the sustainable, repeatable, long-term growth that I'm guessing you're looking for.

Preview text

The preview text can often be overlooked, but it's still a key part of determining the open rate. The clever ones tend to riff off subject lines. The subject line (from Timberland) was, "Up to 40% off" and for the preview line it was:

👆 **Better Than Their Black Friday Deals** 👆

Preview text has the smallest prominence in the inbox, but it can be really handy if you've got a subject line that's just a little too long. Try breaking it in half and putting it into the preview text. For example, when a sale is ending and there's a set percentage off:

» Subject line: Sale ends soon ⏰ / Preview text: 50% off.

It makes it shorter and makes the point clearer.

How to improve the preview text:

→ Be clear and direct (don't waffle!)

→ Be honest about what's in the email

→ Make it stand out in the reader's inbox

Always be sure to send yourself a proof or a test email before you send it out, so you can see how all three of these things come together.

Remember, the goal of an email isn't to get everyone to open it – just the right people; those people that will click through, make a purchase or stay loyal.

Open rates control how many readers can click through and ultimately buy. Tweaking them for maximum success is a great idea, and, as RAC's Chief Marketing Officer said in the foreword, "It's all about incremental, and often marginal, gains."

We're not looking to double the open rate (because that's incredibly hard to do!), we're trying to make tweaks to increase it little by little.

And just in case I didn't spell it out enough, the three things that impact open rates are:

1. **From name < Don't forget about this one!**

2. **Subject line**

3. **Preview text**

Click rates

Click rates are measured as the number of people who clicked a link. Seems straightforward enough: if you put more links in, more people will click one!

But when you're trying to get readers to take a singular action (like clicking through to make a purchase), it's actually better to reduce the number of different places to click.

Readers will *tend to* click one link in your email and be unlikely to come back for more. So, link stuffing can work against you, especially if there are a lot of competing links that don't serve that Primary Action we spoke about earlier. Social media links in a footer are a good example of this – they can be an important channel, but if they're not key for you, I'd recommend leaving them out to avoid the fat-fingered from clicking to Facebook and getting lost.

Buttons are good. If it's a long email, repeat the button so there's always one on screen (or not too far away) to encourage that click.

Have a go at experimenting with the button size. Depending on the original size, if you increase it a little bit it can be easier for mobile users to click the screen.

How to improve click rates:

→ **Make buttons bigger,** especially if your audience mostly reads your emails on a mobile.

→ **Limit the number of different links** and focus on one Primary Action.

→ **Repeat the button or call-to-action** if it's a long email, so it's easier to click.

What if things don't go right?

The numbers don't always tell you the truth

Context is more important than figures

At the beginning of the coronavirus lockdown in the UK, open rates skyrocketed, as did online shopping. But a sudden boost (or conversely, a sudden drop) doesn't always mean what you think it might.

The wider context can be really helpful to understanding the peaks and troughs in your data.

Typical wisdom would hold that during periods of uncertainty, spending drops, but during the coronavirus lockdown there were quite a few winners – e-commerce being among the biggest beneficiaries.

The same is true with seasonal variance, like how consumers place more orders and spend more in the run up to Christmas.

Depending on the country you're targeting, there can be a cultural element, too, such as the frequency that people get paid. In the US, it's more common to be paid fortnightly, whereas in the UK, people are more likely to receive their salary monthly.

In the UK, luxury brands that target middle to high income earners tend to see more sales coming in during the last week of the month, when most salaried staff are paid.

It's important to step back from the figures and to understand and appreciate the bigger picture. While you can't control marketing forces and contexts, they can help you to build a more informed story about what's happened.

Setting realistic aims

If you aim for a 100% open rate, you'll be deeply disappointed.

A realistic aim should be to beat either your last email campaign results or the recent average. For instance, you could set a goal to *increase clicks by 5%*, and to focus on the button text to do that.

Once you've sent a few campaigns and you're getting results in, it'll be easier to get a grip on what 'normal' looks like, with a view to improving that normal every month and year.

If it's a new campaign, it can be really difficult to predict what will happen. Poppy's Plants hasn't done a Black Friday campaign before, so as we plan how to do it, we could pick an arbitrary *Sell 500 plants target*. Or we could try a *get 20% more than this time last year* goal. And once you've done it once, that's the new benchmark – how can you beat that number?

Clear out deadwood subscribers

If you've emailed someone who hasn't opened a single message in the last 12 months, how likely are they to take action with you? Probably not very.

Unless you're a household name, they might have already forgotten who you are, so it's super important to have a clear out every once in a while, to make sure you're only emailing readers who want to hear from you. By removing 'dead' email addresses, you will boost your open rates long-term.

Power up

Experiment further with A/B testing

I've talked a lot about measuring success and then trying to improve on it. But how do we do that? Experimentation.

In an A/B test, you send out two emails and find out which one performs better. Let's do an example.

We want to test if we can offer a more expensive plant than we'd normally feature in the Poppy's Plants newsletter, in order to boost the Average Order Value.

→ Version A features a plant at around the £25 mark (which is what we normally sell at).

→ Version B features a more expensive plant, at around £40.

We want to see if the same number of people click through on the higher price point and then buy.

→ Version A goes to 10% of our 1,000 subscribers (100 people).

→ Version B goes to 10% of our 1,000 subscribers (100 people).

→ We then wait for a few hours to see which one will win.

→ Version A had an open rate of 35% and a click rate of 20%.

→ Version B had an open rate of 40% and a click rate of 25%.

→ Version B is the winner, as it has more clicks. Version B is then sent out to the remaining 80% of our 1,000 subscribers (800 people).

From this, we can see that we got more clicks from a higher price point, which is good for the bottom line. Going forward, we'll adapt this and feature plants at around £40.

A/B tests are a very common feature on email platforms, and they can help you to learn and then implement what you've learned in one fell swoop. They do, however, require a little bit of planning, as you need to have an idea about what to test.

If you want to learn more about email metrics and testing, I've got some useful courses at sendbetter.email/courses.

For those of you who want to be more scientific about testing, I highly recommend the book *Trustworthy Online Controlled Experiments: A Practical Guide to A/B Testing*, by Ron Kahavi, Diane Tang and Ya Xu, the three minds behind experimentation and optimisation at Microsoft, Google and LinkedIn. It's quite dense, so if you're starting out, I'd suggest the YouTube channel *Crash Course* instead. They have a free module on statistics, which is very easy to digest.

> You can download an A/B testing pack to help you pick what you want to test and formalise your results at sendbetter.email/resources. I've built a free tool at https://junction.email that helps email marketers log and analyse their results. It's overkill if you're starting out, but if you're looking to seriously experiment, it can help you understand results and share them with others.

WRAPPING IT UP

In this section, we've covered:

- ✓ How to help your readers – giving more than you take to build a helpful relationship with your audience.

- ✓ Planning emails – from customer personas through to the automation sequences you need to think about.

- ✓ Defining success – ensuring emails are being measured, what those open rates mean and how to improve them.

In the next section, we'll look to build on these brilliant basics to grow your audience, say hello and promote your list.

SECTION TWO – GROW YOUR AUDIENCE

Now that you've got a good idea on where you want to go and how you can help the reader, let's look at how to get more readers signed up to your list.

In this section, I'll go through:

> » Signing up – how to make it easy, quick and painless.

> » Saying hello – strike while the iron's hot and remind your readers who you are in the coming days and weeks.

> » Promoting your list – how to get scale on acquiring new readers.

Chapter 4: Signing up

Converting website visitors into subscribers isn't easy. Even on the best web pages, you're looking at a 2% to 3% conversion rate.

That means 97 people in every 100 bugger off, potentially never to be seen again. So, trying to capture their email address is super important for keeping in touch.

The easiest way to do this is to have some kind of sidebar or form on a page to receive email addresses, which will then upload to your email platform.

Let's go back to our Poppy's Plants example.

We've got 1,000 subscribers and our email programme generates £15k a year. That means every email address is worth £15.

This is a reasonable gauge to use when planning how to spend your marketing budget. If you could buy a piece of software for £30 a year that would double sign ups, you'd only need two extra people (worth £15) to sign up who wouldn't have otherwise done so for it to be worth it.

Making it easy to sign up is key. Asking for just an email address is the gold standard. For every additional piece of data (like first name, company name, phone number, etc.), expect a drop of about 5%. HubSpot is an example where requesting a free report gives you a sign-up form that asks for a huge amount of information.

Take a look at Example 13 over the page. Imagine having to fill that in on most websites you visit, it'd be exhausting!

Let's think about what we're trying to do with email marketing for a minute. We're trying to get readers to sign up so we can communicate with them directly.

Another goal could be to get qualified leads, involving getting lots of information so you can work out whether the lead is a good one. This is mostly used in B2B, which is companies that only sell to other companies rather than to the general public, as well as in the marketing of high-ticket consumer items, such as cars or financial products.

Download Now

First Name *

Last Name *

Email *

Phone Number *

Company Name *

How many employees work there? *

- Please Select -   ▼

Website URL *

☐ **Subscribe to HubSpot's marketing blog**

Example 13 – HubSpot sign-up form.

HubSpot is trying to do both. They're a big company and will know this format will really hurt the number of people who sign up, but they are banking on those people being much more likely to become customers, and with the additional information like company size, they can talk to their readers in a more tailored way.

I strongly recommend just asking for an email address and a first name. If you wanted to, you could ask readers for more information at a later date. This approach of asking for just two pieces of information will boost the number of people who sign up.

How to say hi...

Once you've got a new sign up, it's time to make them feel loved. They're in the mood the minute they click subscribe or sign up.

A welcome email is a message that goes out as soon as they sign up. It's automatic, meaning you don't have to do anything, and the reader gets a nice introduction right into their inbox.

I talk about how to personalise these emails in Section Three – Chapter 8, *Working Smarter*, so you might want to use these two sections together. Getting the salutation right will have a big impact on how the reader feels about you.

Older readers prefer "Dear <Title> <Surname>", while younger audiences prefer a less formal salutation "Hello <First name>".

Having worked with brands on both sides of the age spectrum, this can be key to the reader feeling like you 'get them'. Your reader persona can help you narrow down the age or type of reader you want to attract.

In the next chapter, we'll look at how a welcome email can turn into a welcome sequence, and I'll show you some templates on how to make this work for your business.

Now that you know how valuable each email is, hopefully you can see the importance of getting them. So, now you need to entice your visitors into giving you their email address. There are 2 ways of doing this:

1. Lead magnet – where they get a thing, then a newsletter.

A lead magnet is a free document, course or something of value for the price of an email address. This is a common way to get an interested person to give you their details so you can email them later.

2. Newsletter IS the magnet.

Instead of giving a lead magnet away and adding Jess to the fortnightly newsletter, make the newsletter the magnet itself.

Attract the right prospects with lead magnets

As the name suggests, these are downloadable documents that are specifically for your leads. They draw leads in 'like a magnet'. So, "The plants you need to brighten your flat" free eBook will definitely appeal to our Jess reader persona.

This could be in the form of a report with helpful insights, a template that Jess can fill in to help her reach a goal or a series of short emails to provoke thought or provide some quick tips.

And just like a magnet, it will repel the people who don't want plants or who don't live in a flat. Always be mindful that repelling the 'wrong' people is the right move.

Let's have a look at a couple of examples (see the email flowchart 1 on the next page). We'll go through this particular example in greater detail in the last chapter, *Putting it All Together.*

All flowcharts featured in this book can be downloaded from
sendbetter.email/flowcharts

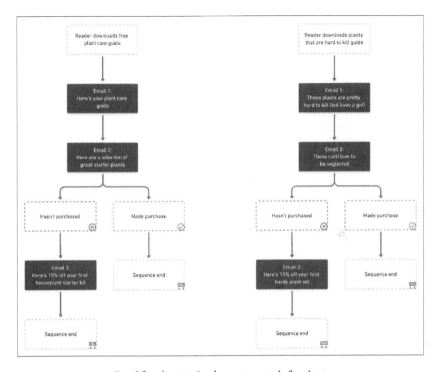

Email flowchart 1 – Lead magnet example flowchart.

What should a lead magnet be?

Short and sweet.

It should demonstrate your expertise in your field, without giving the game away. Ideally less than ten pages, it should be a teaser (after all, it's free!) and should seek to establish you in the mind of the reader as knowing what you're on about, while getting a feel for who you are and what you believe in.

"Where do I even start?" I hear you ask. It can be difficult, especially if you've not done it before or don't have the budget for a graphic designer to make it look pretty.

I'd highly recommend looking into Beacon, a website for beginners that's dedicated to making lead magnets. They have templates, and it's super easy to get started. They'll even sort out a lead magnet form for you and help you to make it look pretty.

> Have a look and explore the templates and how they might streamline the creation of a lead magnet process at sendbetter.email/beacon.

Practical or template?

If you can solve a problem in practical terms, gold stars for you. Your Jess will thank you for giving her the shortcuts she needs to make her flat look nicer with some green friends.

If you've got a template for Jess to use herself, all the better. Obviously, this is easier for professional service-type businesses, but Jess might appreciate having a free download that will help her note down all her plants, their locations and their watering schedules.

Helping readers to solve a problem should be the name of the game, and anything that can also demonstrate your experience or show off your previous clients or case studies is an added bonus.

Remember, the free download should **help your reader**, but it should also lead them back to you **helping them more**. Whether that's through purchasing a course, a session or something else, the main goal is to convert readers into customers.

Regular newsletters

It's common for readers to give up their email address to get a freebie. Most of the time, this process of redeeming a free download also adds them to a newsletter. You'll see this tried and tested model all over the internet, and it works.

But there's an additional way you can recruit people – making the newsletter the freebie itself. Pack it full of content and encourage people to sign up to it.

It's often most successful on a front page or in a sidebar – or on a dedicated page all to itself.

I used a great example earlier in the book from Spaghetti Agency, which runs a newsletter called the *Friday Digital Roundup*. This is a product by itself. It's free to readers and carries small adverts for the company's paid products.

Its main aim isn't to sell, rather it gives readers a bit of a chuckle on a Friday morning – and the community buzz that's built around it provides really strong social proof that it's worth signing up for.

They recap the funniest news stories from across social media. This entertains readers (a great goal!), as well as proving they've got their finger on the pulse of different social networks.

By making the newsletter such a stand-out product by itself, people want to sign up without an incentive. This is the gold standard, where readers willingly sign up to receive promotional emails because they actively want to receive them – and those open rates and engagements (and ultimately, sales) will be sky high.

That's what I do for my weekly newsletter Emails Explained. It has its own one-page website (EmailsExplained.com) and is a very simple example of the newsletter being the freebie. (See Example 14 on the next page.) The newsletter gives ideas and inspiration on email marketing. It also features on my website inboxhero.co.uk, but having Emails Explained be its own product helps it to stand out and be seen as more than "just my company newsletter".

So, now you've got your 'carrot' of choice, it's time to talk about what to do once they've signed up.

You can sign up to my email newsletter by visiting
www.emailsexplained.com

Example 14 – Screenshot from EmailsExplained.com.

Set expectations

Sending out a weekly email? Let the readers know that when they sign up. I know I've harped on about this before (and no doubt will do again before we're finished!) in the Keep Going Commandment, but it's super important to make sure people know what they're getting upfront.

If a reader downloads a free PDF that will sign them up to your regular newsletter, tell them so they expect it. Otherwise, they might be confused about why they're getting your emails (as they might not remember you) or, in the worst-case scenario, mark you as spam.

If you've got some great examples of past newsletters, link to them. Use a line like, "Sign up to our weekly Plant Parent newsletter, where you'll get tips on how to care for your green pets – read some back issues here >>." The reader can then view some examples to see if the newsletter is something they want to receive.

If you promise a weekly email about plant care and then send out a daily sales blast, the reader is probably going to quickly hit the unsubscribe button.

Set expectations. Then deliver on them.

Quality over quantity

Quality is always more important than quantity. The same is true for the type of subscriber you get.

We've got a bunch of Jesses already signed up. They're a great fit, they're engaged in opening emails and they're ready or almost ready to buy.

Like I said above, it's the **RIGHT** type of person vs the **NUMBER** of people.

We want more people like Jess. That isn't the same as *we want more people.*

Once you're targeting the Jesses of the world, there's another way you can try to weed out the 'bad apples', the people who never open their emails: **double opt-in.**

There's a question in MailChimp (and most email platforms) – a simple tick box whether to use double opt-in, where an email is sent to the reader to confirm they've signed up. This gets rid of a lot of people, who for some reason or another couldn't be bothered to switch to their mailbox and click the link. It also weeds out fake email addresses and typos.

So, those readers that do click the button tend to be more engaged.

To take the opposing view, this creates a hurdle.

Imagine you're Jess, our reader, who is on her mobile while waiting for the bus, which is about two minutes away:

» *Oh, yes, I want to download that free guide.*

» Enters email address.

» *"Thanks for signing up, check your inbox and click the link."*

» Closes browser.

» Opens mail app.

» Clicks link.

» *"Thanks for confirming your email, check your inbox for the free guide."*

» Closes browser.

» Opens mail app.

» Clicks link.

» Reads guide.

The bus arrived between stages 7 and 8 and Jess had to switch to her mobile ticket app. And then, thanks to the shortage of seats, she promptly forgot about the free guide. However, as she was SUPER keen on getting it, as soon as she got to work, she checked her inbox and clicked the link.

I appreciate this is a bit of a drawn-out example, but it's exactly what a double opt-in sequence looks like.

Yes, it gets more engaged people, purely by virtue of the fact they've got to jump through a few hoops to be on the list. So, better engagement but slightly fewer people – which would you prefer?

If at all possible, try to follow up with readers who do sign up but never make it as far as clicking "confirm" – it might be that they need another nudge, or that they had to stand the whole way on their commute to work.

Single opt-in

I'm a big fan of single opt-in (where the reader signs up and then voila, they're on the list), but this only works if there's something else that checks the email addresses are valid (normally done by your email platform), and there's a special sequence for people who never engage.

This 'sunset' sequence can improve your open rates, simply by removing all the people who never engage with your emails. If your readers haven't opened an email from you in the last 90 days, it's unlikely they'll do so again.

Yes, it is yet another sequence to set up, but it keeps the amount of dead wood from increasing too much.

Do what's easiest for you now. Double opt-ins are favoured by email platforms, as they reduce the number of people who complain they never signed up. But once you've got your feet under the desk of your email marketing, sign up with a test email address and see what the experience feels like from a reader's point of view. Then explore how you can make things smoother.

Pop ups

Pop ups come in 2 flavours:

1. Incredibly annoying
2. Slightly annoying

I'm loath to recommend popups, because when they're not set up properly, they can be irritatingly fiddly to get rid of for mobile users. Saying that, they can be an incredible source of email sign ups – even from the very beginning.

The main things a popup must do is be easy to fill in, clear in the call-to-action, easily closed and offer something useful.

Here are some examples of the good (and the bad!)

Example 15 – Nice popup, a not so great way to exit.

I love this popup because it's clear and has a compelling reason to sign up. The only thing that doesn't really jive with me is the way to exit: "No, thanks. I like my marketing poopy."

If someone's not interested, they're not interested. Shaming them because of that is at best counterintuitive and at worst mildly offensive.

A "No, thanks" would have been fine.

Example 16 – "No thanks, I'll just wing it."

Example 17 – "Nah, I don't want to be a successful entrepreneur."

Some more examples of 'negging' – the idea of shaming customers to not click the close button – can be found at the Cruellest Opt Out Tumblr page: https://cruelestoptouts.tumblr.com

The example below is nice and clear, and there's only one field to fill in and one button. It gets a big thumbs up from me.

Example 18 – A great popup example.

Offering a discount for signing up can be a great way to get extra readers (and customers!), but be careful to check that this doesn't 'cannibalise sales' – i.e., that you're not offering a discount to people who were going to buy anyway, thus slashing your profit.

Example 19 – Sign up for a discount.

The example below is a great way to promote an eBook – there are two fields, one button, simple imagery and an easily identifiable X button to close – this is how all popups should look.

Example 20 – Sign up for a free eBook.

Just because it's an annoying popup doesn't mean you can't let your brand voice and some quirky charm shine through.

Example 21 – Entertaining popups that poke fun at themselves.

Check with your email platform or the person who runs your website what the best way is to add your email subscribers. If you're using WordPress to power your website, there are a number of plugins that can help with the technical side and simplify the sign-up process.

Tracking people

If you set your tech up properly, you'll be able to see where people come from. In MailChimp, this is how you set different lead magnets up to send out different emails.

This can be a good way to work out where people are coming from to get onto your list.

For example, if you have a sign up form you only promote on Twitter and another you only promote on Facebook, you can gauge or measure the percentage of people coming from these two separate mediums.

If you're starting out, I'd skip over this bit, but when you begin to get going it can help you to focus on the channels that are working and the ones that need a bit more love.

Easy to leave

It sounds counterintuitive, but you also want to help people to leave. If they're not getting value out of what you're sending, that's a shame, but you don't want to keep spamming them.

It's part of the *Ten Email Commandments* we covered earlier, Let Go (Gracefully), where we talked about how there will always be people who leave. It's not the worst thing to happen, it's a good thing.

It might be them. Our priorities are constantly changing, so that new car purchase might be thrown into chaos if a spouse loses their job. Or a house purchase and all the interests that come with that might be postponed if there's an unexpected pregnancy.

Sometimes, it's you. If people are leaving in their droves (and big spikes tend to give the game away), they're telling you something, and it isn't good.

Take it on the chin, read any comments they might have left when unsubscribing and try to see the positive and take action. If people are leaving and saying they don't want to get your emails anymore, could you be sending them too often? Does your mail out not match what they expected? Are you accidentally sending the wrong email to the wrong people?

If that is the case, then you're reading the right book. Take action on my advice, or, if you're still stumped by what you're seeing, let's get together. We can set up a Power Hour to get to the root of your problem, and I can give some actionable advice on how to resolve it. Head to sendbetter.email/powerhour and let's get started.

Chapter 5: Saying hello

So, you now have your lovely, shiny subscriber, and they are all ready to receive your emails . . . now let's take a look at your welcome sequence.

What is a welcome sequence?

A welcome sequence will be one of the first interactions a reader will have with your business.

So, it's super important to get this set up right, and I've got a great template at the end of this section that you need to implement, today!

Even if you do nothing else in this book, the welcome sequence is the quickest win that can move the needle the most.

Welcome sequences come in a variety of flavours, but normally, three to five emails are sent after the reader does something:

» Signs up to a mailing list (the traditional welcome sequence, and what we'll focus on in this chapter).

» Purchases a product (a post-purchase sequence).

» Downloads a free product (a follow-up sequence).

» Goes to the checkout but doesn't buy (an abandon-basket sequence).

I've worked with larger businesses on more specific automations, like a follow-up sequence that a customer receives after they change their address (with a view to offering new home-related products). These can be niche but lucrative, if you identify at exactly what point people are most likely to make a purchase.

Saying hello is just what civilised people do. Read on and prioritise getting a welcome sequence set up.

Why welcome sequences work

In every case study I've seen, and with every brand I've worked with, having a welcome sequence pays off.

There's an example template at the end of this section. Work through it, upload three into your email platform provider and set it to live.

This shouldn't take much more than an hour, and the results might surprise you.

Typically, readers who have received a welcome sequence will have higher open and click rates. There are a few theories as to why:

1.   Readers get used to seeing you in their inbox. As they keep opening your emails, a habit is built. So, the next email is more likely to be opened. And the next. And you see where this is going . . .

2.   When readers open your emails, they're telling their mailbox provider that they're interesting and to prioritise them, which means your messages are less likely to end up in their junk box or be filtered out.

3.   Readers remember you right now. Building on that helps them remember you for longer. It sounds a bit ridiculous, but readers can be fickle beasts. With a whole internet to choose from, they've decided on you. In a couple of months, they might forget that, so it's a good idea to strike while the iron is hot.

Take a look at the case study over the page, where I helped the speech-writing company Speechy convert casual browsers into paying customers.

Offer value not discounts

Discounts always have a place. They really do. They get people moving. You only have to look at Black Friday to realise that if you advertise a 50%-off sale, you'll get a lot more customers.

...Cont' on page 110

CASE STUDY #1: Speechy

I worked with the company Speechy, which helps wedding parties with writing and delivering their speeches.

From pre-built templates to fully customised packages, Heidi and her team help brides, grooms, fathers of the bride, etc., to write speeches that everyone will remember. They also provide coaching on how to deliver them.

The welcome sequence is a key marketing activity for Speechy, converting casual browsers to receiving speech tips on specific wedding role pages or blog posts.

After a few seconds of inactivity, or when the website thinks the reader might be about to leave, they will see this popup:

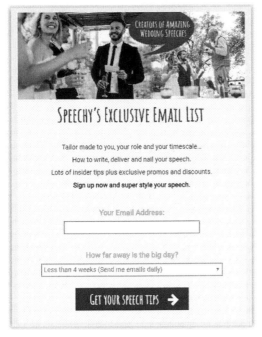

Example 22 – Speechy popup form.

It's a simple form. Readers only enter their email address and then how far away their wedding is (so their emails are spaced out appropriately) – setting that expectation right from the outset.

The website knows what page the reader was on when the popup was filled out, so sends the most appropriate one of nine different welcome sequences, from groom, to mother of the bride, to same sex weddings.

The welcome sequence features five emails, all containing a lot of good advice, alongside client testimonials, discounts and product promotions. The welcome sequence gives more than it takes, but business is about that free exchange, and it works well.

In the first few months of the sequence launching, Speechy saw lots of new subscribers and brought in automated sales. While a few people may have bought anyway, the vast majority of purchasers didn't buy straight away, were warmed up and then felt convinced enough to put cash in the till.

This case study demonstrates how easy it can be to pick the low-hanging fruit; people who are browsing but might not be quite ready to pull out their credit cards just yet.

By engaging them through a new subscriber welcome sequence, trust is built and experience proved, which can help to overcome initial purchasing objections, especially on emotive subjects (like weddings!) or on higher ticket or more personalised services (like speech writing).

This isn't the same kind of impulse purchase as picking up a Twix at the checkout, these are purchases that need a bit of logic and emotion to get over the line.

For more on the head-heart dynamic in sales and marketing, I wholeheartedly recommend the book *Watertight Marketing* by Bryony Thomas, who explains retention and loyalty as if prospects are water, with business owners turning on marketing 'taps' to flow into buckets.

Here's some more from Speechy founder Heidi Ellert-McDermott:

Speechy targets so many different demographics – from grooms getting married next week, to mothers of the bride planning for weddings over a year away, and everyone in between!

I knew an email marketing list would be helpful in converting our 85k users who visit the site every year into clients, but I was overwhelmed at the prospect of setting up an effective email list that could provide engaging offers to all our different customer groups.

Jon was a godsend. He showed me how to segment our users into email groups with a simple popup involving just two questions: "What's your role at the wedding?" (with a drop-down box of options) and "When is the wedding date?" (Again, with drop-down options, ranging from "within a week" to "over a year to go.")

From there, we could easily segment the users into their appropriate roles (e.g., best man or bride, etc.), and then use the wedding date to schedule the emails to be delivered at appropriate times.

Speechy obviously needed to keep in touch with those people whose weddings were still a long way off, so we developed a plan to create 5 emails per role, each delivering different advice and a new discount/ promotion – i.e., a double win.

   ✓ *First email: an introduction to the team.*

   ✓ *Second: how to plan your speech.*

   ✓ *Third: how to write your speech.*

   ✓ *Fourth: how to deliver your speech.*

   ✓ *Fifth: Speechy's testimonials and final big hitter discount.*

Once we had the format for each email, I simply needed to tweak the imagery and text slightly to take into account the different role of the recipient. Jon set everything up on MailChimp, and the process felt

> *extremely easy from my point of view. Considering the complexity of the project, it was also extremely good value for money.*
>
> *A year after the campaign was installed onto our site, I can safely say it was money well spent. I continue to draw on Jon's expertise and hope to update our e-marketing offering with further innovation that Jon has alerted us to.*

But it always comes at a cost. That discount level eats into the pure profit. The heavier the discount, the less profit you make. The base item costs the same, and so does the price of the labour, electricity and postage.

Where it makes sense, I'd always recommend using "value add" offers more than discounting.

Here's what I mean:

Poppy's Plants by Post sends out flowers in a box that will fit through your letterbox every month. The yearly membership is £100, and it costs £50 for all the direct expenses (packaging, postage, the flowers, address labels, etc.) – so the profit on each membership is £50. Let's ignore overheads, we're just working through some napkin maths here.

Say we want to increase the number of customers we have. For this example, we'll look at two different options:

1. **Dropping the price by 25%.**

2. **Increasing the length of a subscription by 25%.**

The customer would see these as either '25% off' or '3 extra months free.'

1. Discounting – Dropping the price by 25%.

The year's membership is now £75, down from £100. Our costs are still £50, so our profit is £25 overall, half of what it was in the original example. The discount eats directly into the profit and can very often overwhelm a business if it gets out of control.

As previously mentioned, I worked with a wool shop that started giving 10% off on orders through its new newsletter. It was so popular that the shop, which runs on very small margins to compete with online stores, made no money, and even lost money on each order.

2. Value added offer – Increasing the length of a subscription by 25%.

The year's membership is now 15 months, not 12, but the price remains £100. The costs will go up by 25% (as these are direct expenses, and if the membership goes on 25% longer, so do the costs), which means they are now £62.50, making the total profit £37.50.

This example shows how the customer feels they're receiving the same thing (in both scenarios they get three months free), but the business owner is making more profit on the second option because costs are (or at least should be!) lower than the price paid.

It depends very much on the nature of the business and the specific positioning of the brand in relation to its competitors. If the biggest consideration of the customers in general is cost, and the business has a USP of not being undercut, then discounting is very hard to avoid.

But for firms where price is one of many rather than the sole consideration, a value-added offer can be a really good way to preserve profit, and in both examples, you can still use the same "3 months free" offer, which can be really useful for subscription or service-based brands.

Welcome sequence templates

Welcome sequences are all about occupying the reader's front of mind thinking (or at least front of inbox!).

They've come to Poppy's Plants because they have a specific problem: their flat looks dull and they want to brighten it up.

A short welcome sequence giving them free tips and some additional reasons to buy (free shipping or a free plant when you spend over £75).

If you want to go all out, you could have a new welcome sequence for each of the ways people have of getting onto your email list. This might be one for an eBook linking back to it, one for those who sign up on your homepage and another for those who make a purchase. This is exactly what the aforementioned Speechy did; it had nine separate welcome sequences and you got a tailored set of emails depending on the page you signed up on.

In this example, Jess has just signed up to download the free *"The plants you need to brighten your flat"* eBook.

→ **Email #1:** The main goal here is to get the reader to download the guide they asked for.

Subject line:	Here's your guide to brightening your flat with plants.
Copy:	Hi Jess, You can download your guide at: [LINK] I'm Poppy and I run Poppy's Plants, a high street, family-run shop in Bristol. My house is teeming with green friends, and no matter how big or small your living space, you've always got room for a plant friend. I'll be sending you a few more tips over the coming days, and then you'll receive my fortnightly newsletter. If you've got any questions, don't hesitate to email me or phone on 0117 555 0123. Happy planting, Poppy
Button:	Download your guide

→ **Email #2:** The main goal here is to follow up with some additional tips – but for the sake of those readers who read the guide and made a purchase, we can (in email platforms that connect with e-commerce) exclude people who have made a purchase. It makes for a more seamless experience, and it's explored further in Section Three – Chapter 7, *Why Data is King.*

Subject line:	Did you find some great plants for your flat?
Copy:	Hi Jess, How did you get on with your Guide to Indoor Plants for Flats? [LINK] When I lived in London, I shared a house and had a tiny room. But this little Venus Fly Trap kept me company and the flower it sends up is beautiful. And so, my passion for flowers began. If you're looking for hardy plants (that like being a bit neglected), I'd recommend these succulents: [LINKS and PHOTOS] For plants that love the warmth and humidity of your bathroom, check out these beauties: [LINKS and PHOTOS] Again, if you've got any questions, don't hesitate to email me or phone on 0117 555 0123. Happy planting, Poppy
Button:	Check out these easy to look after plants >>

→ **Email #3:** The main goal here is to set the scene, follow up on any specific queries, and then add the user to get the main newsletter. Again, excluding readers who are now customers.

Subject line:	Need a hand picking out the right plant for your flat?
Copy:	Hi Jess, Did you find the plant you were looking for? You can check out the guide I sent you a few days ago at: [LINK] And if you have any questions at all, just reply to this email and I'll help you find the perfect plant for you and your flat. Happy planting, Poppy
Button:	Click here to reply

Even a short, three-email sequence like the one featured here can build trust, impart wisdom and, ultimately, overcome any objections to make the sale. And this can happen automatically, every minute of every day. Magic, eh?

Write it on your to-do list right now. I'll wait.

No, seriously, I'll wait.

Then plan it and start sending it out when readers sign up. It doesn't have to be amazing at first, you can always make it better later. But done will always beat perfect!

Chapter 6: Promoting your list

Now that we have our sign-up form and our welcome sequence in place, it's time to promote your list so you get more subscribers.

Putting people off

Thinking back to our reader persona exercise from Section One – Chapter 2: *Planning Emails*, we can imagine the ideal reader who'd be great to sign up, but sometimes it's useful to bear in mind the opposite – people whom we don't want to subscribe.

I recall signing up to a newsletter that turned into a nightmare. This was a respected guy in the copywriting field, and I thought it would be a good resource to keep developing my writing skills.

Boy, was I wrong! This guy's so overtly American the email notification sound might as well have been *The Star-Spangled Banner*.

He's quite a lot of a racist *"and I won't apologise for it!"*, and the whole ethos of the newsletter is to shame people who don't subscribe to his world view, boast about how successful he is (or pretends to be) and point out why he's the bomb and everyone else sucks.

Surprisingly, I'm not actually talking about Trump, but this guy could give the Don a run for his money!

So, you want to repel the people who don't fit the reader persona exercise we did earlier (or are the antithesis of them). I obviously wasn't the right fit for this guy, and I'd never buy from him. So, if he'd been upfront, I would have been successfully repelled and wouldn't have signed up.

I know this might seem counterintuitive, especially as every marketing guru says, "Build your email list high and fast", but think about it as trying to keep your focus on the people you might be able to convert. With that in mind, don't be afraid of explaining who you are and what you stand for at the sign-up point – it might turn some people off, but that's a good thing. There's no point preaching to those who can never be converted because they've already made up their mind.

If you're a nightclub owner, do you want to get an email address so you can communicate with the little old couple in their retirement bungalow? You *can*, but that doesn't always mean you *should*, and repelling the wrong people is always a smart move – and will often save you money.

The king of this is, and I begrudgingly use him as an example again, President Trump. He repels everyone who's not in his core fan base. But that also means his fans are SUPER FANS.

They'll queue for hours in all weathers, because he speaks to only them. He doesn't give a toffee what anyone who's not 'on his team' thinks (part of his charm, I'm sure) and that creates a stronger bond with his key base.

Not that I'd recommend becoming Trump, but you get the idea. Speak to your tribe and repel those who won't ever be a good fit – it's about the RIGHT people, not the NUMBER of people.

Ask questions – does this sound like you?

A useful way to weed out the faux readers and build an instant connection is by using identifying questions:

→ *Want to brighten up your flat with some greenery?*

→ *Looking for some easy-to-maintain plants?*

→ *Trying to figure out which room a plant should live in?*

→ ***Then sign up below and get the free guide and our fortnightly newsletter.***

By screening out people who don't live in flats, or those who already know the ideal conditions of plants, you can build quite a precise image of the reader persona – and then a good copywriter can help you really bring it to life.

I'd suggest keeping the questions positive, so, "Looking for some easy-to-maintain plants?" rather than, "Did you kill the last plants you bought?" – unless the negativity fits in with your brand.

Keeping up with the Joneses

It's a good tactic to show that your newsletter is in demand by pointing out that other people are interested in it – this is often called social proof.

If you say, "Join over 500 other green-fingered beginners for the fortnightly Plant Parent newsletter", I'll know that other people have signed up and have liked it enough to stay.

If you can get quotes from your audience like, "This newsletter is the bees knees" and "I couldn't imagine getting plant inspiration from anywhere else" – it's a really powerful way to help potential readers overcome the feeling they're signing up to get spammed.

And with newsletters becoming more popular, it's important to try and stand out, even from competitors. Although I'm guessing (and hoping!) that your website and marketing generally makes this clear.

Where do your readers hang out?

How can you get your newsletter form in front of them?

So, you've crafted your reader persona, Jess.

How do we get the Plant Parent newsletter in front of her?

We've got to work out where she lives. Not in the stalkery, leave-roses-on-the-doorstep way, but where does Jess go, either online or in person, where we can advertise in front of her?

Does she get her news from a specific kind of magazine? She might subscribe to some other newsletters from bigger brands – are there any inroads we could make there?

Does she give to charities, and can we partner with them to advertise to all the Jesses? Perhaps even expanding it slightly to childfree women aged 20 to 40, living in cities.

Inevitably, there are two major players in this kind of thing: Facebook and Google. I'm not particularly versed in either, so I'd recommend locating an expert in each and fixing a plan.

The blogs Jess reads

Do you know any blogs that Jess might read? A good way to try and understand this is by asking your core customers what blogs they read.

If there are lots of overlaps, or several blogs that you might be able to reach out to, why not consider a guest blog?

This is where you blog under your own name, but on someone else's site. There's an art to doing this well, but if you can build some traction and if what you're writing about will resonate with the blog's audience, you should be a shoe-in.

The podcasts Jess listens to

The same example can be used for podcasts; getting a guest interview slot can help you elevate your profile to the Jesses that haven't heard of you.

Keep pitching – work on the elevator pitch for your newsletter, mainly for podcast appearances, but also for that dinner party where you meet a Jess that might be interested.

Keep it to under 30 seconds, a quick recap of who you are, what you do and how you help people – with the vital ending: sign up for my newsletter.

Posting to your peers

Never underestimate sharing your newsletter with your network. If you've got Facebook friends, Twitter followers or Instagram stalkers, it's time to share your newsletter.

You can also do this with every new send. Most email platforms will give you a web link so you can share your email. Posting about it on social media can generate some buzz from the people who already follow you and prompt them to subscribe, but it can also build momentum from those who don't yet know you to get involved.

Promoting through partnerships

Instead of reaching your readers, why not try and target the readers of other newsletters? This is where relationships can come in handy.

No doubt you'll have heard about the four dreaded letters: GDPR. And this can sometimes be a reason why businesses are reluctant to combine their email marketing efforts, but in practice, you don't need to fear them.

The three key things you need to do:

1. Make sure people sign up themselves (this is called explicit opt-in).
2. Make sure you protect their data (by using an email platform).
3. Make sure you give people a way to leave (by using an unsubscribe link).

Obviously, it's a lot more complex than this, but if you follow these three best practices, you won't have any sleepless nights, and so long as partnerships follow these rules, too, you're A-OK to move ahead. Don't let the GDPR fear brigade stop you from thinking outside the box.

Business partnerships

A business partnership is where two (or more) businesses get together and send some content out together. This normally happens with local chambers of commerce, but it will also happen where there's a natural complement, such as wedding vendors, mortgage lenders and financial advisors.

For Poppy's Plants, this could mean connecting up with the local pottery store. Plants have to live somewhere, and a good partnership would see Poppy's Plants team up with and promote the pottery store, who will then promote Poppy's Plants.

Even if it's just a banner advert in each other's emails, it can be a good way to build business relationships, be strategically useful and benefit both companies.

Think about all the emails you already receive from companies. Would any of them make for a good collaborative partner? If you're an accountant, a good partner might be a tax advisor. Think similar – you might be indirect competitors but not looking at the same group of customers.

Sit down and make a list of ten companies that are either local or competitors further afield that would make a good partnership, where you both promote the list of the other.

For Poppy's Plants, we're looking at:

» Local florist

» Nearby garden centre (and possibly chain of garden centres)

» Local hardware store

» Local pottery store

» Local corner shop

» Nearby hardware store (and chain)

» Local B2C businesses

» Nearby events businesses

» Nearby office blocks

» Online stationary company

Google Maps can be your friend here. Look at the businesses near you. Would any of them be a good fit as a complementary or indirect competitor?

Reach out to them.

An example email template would be:

Subject line:	I wondered if we could partner up?
Copy:	Hi {Owner's Name}, My name is Poppy, and I run the local plant store. I was looking at {businesses in the local area} to find local mutual business partnerships. I was wondering if you'd be willing to do some cross-promotion, where I'd tell my {customers/clients} about how you might help them, in exchange for the reverse. It wouldn't cost anything at all and might bring benefit to both our businesses. I'd love to have a coffee with you to chat through the idea, or you can call me on 0117 555 0123. Many thanks, Poppy
Call-to-action:	Reply and book appointment.

Make a list and reach out. Do it, now!

Targeting the competition

Unfortunately, you can't reach out and see who has signed up to your competitor's email programme, but you can get a sense of who they are by signing up yourself (with a separate personal email account if you don't want to look like you're snooping).

How they speak to their readers and the offers they use can give you an idea of who their customers are and inspire some ideas.

Roping in your existing clients

Some brands let their customers become affiliates in a paid, word-of-mouth campaign, and this can be super effective. Imagine your best customers getting paid to send you more leads, and only having to cough up a referral fee when money hits the till.

The UK energy company Bulb.co.uk does a great customer affiliate scheme, where if you encourage your friends and family to switch energy providers, you both get a £50 credit.

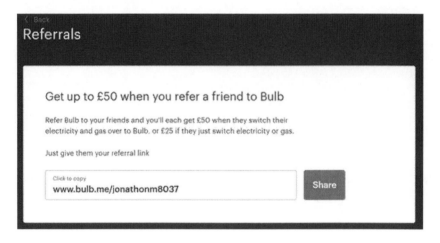

Example 23 – Referrals can be a powerful way to grow.

Thinking outside the box when it comes to promoting your list can work really well. But thinking inside the box is the best place to start. It boils down to two questions:

1. Where are your readers hanging out?

2. How can you get your sign-up box in front of them?

WRAPPING IT UP

In this section, we've looked at:

✓ How readers can sign up – from lead magnets to newsletters and popups, setting expectations and how to let readers go.

✓ Getting off on the right foot – what welcome sequences are, why you should offer value rather than discounts, and some templates.

✓ How to promote your list – finding out where your audience hangs out and encouraging them to sign up.

In the next section, we're going to look at the last three jigsaw pieces, where we take our readers and convert them into customers. Now we've got our solid foundations, and the audience is growing, it's time to turn more of them into paying clients.

SECTION THREE – CONVERT MORE READERS

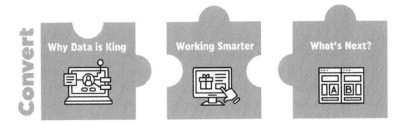

Now that you've got the basics set up, and you've got people on the list, what now?

It's time to turn readers into customers, and we can do this in three steps.

In this section, we will talk about:

» Why Data is King – why you need it, what to collect and how to protect it.

» Working Smarter – what to do with the data you've already got and how to work smarter (not harder!).

» What's Next? – converting a reader into a customer is great. Now turn them into a repeat customer or an advocate.

Chapter 7: Why data is king

There's a saying now that data is more valuable than oil. And the reason for this is that the more useful data you – as the business – possess, the more efficient you can make things for your lovely readers. This means they'll see more relevant things and will be more likely to make a purchase.

The more useful the data (and I'm talking about the things that will help you make the sale, not irrelevant data) and the more targeted you can be, the better conversion rate you'll get, and, ultimately, the more money you'll make from doing the same or less promotional activity.

What data do I need?

What is personal data?

I know this is going to be super boring, but before we talk about how to use data in new and cool ways, we have to be clear on what data is. And yes, I'm going to have to (very briefly) talk about GDPR again. I'm sorry in advance. If you already have a vague concept of what data is, feel free to skip ahead to, "How are you protecting it?"

Data isn't something you can touch and feel.

You can feel the paper it's printed on or the screen it's displayed on, but you can't pour it through your fingers. It has heaps of value, but it's 'intangible', as the accountants will say.

Which is why it can be a bit confusing.

In the way we're talking about it, data is simply all the different pieces of information about people or businesses. It can be in any and all formats, from digital to printed, to handwritten notes to read out over the phone.

Examples of different pieces of data are:

>> Name

>> Address

>> Number of orders

>> Items purchased

>> Email address

When the GDPR came into force in 2018, it meant that there were extra laws on Personally Identifiable Information. This just means pieces of data that might identify someone.

Let's take the previous list of example data pieces and have a look at those that might identify a person:

>> **Name** – yes, this would identify the person.

>> **Address** – yes, this would very likely identify the person.

>> **Number of orders** – no, this is data, but it wouldn't identify the person.

>> **Items purchased** – no, this is data, but it wouldn't identify the person.

>> **Email address** – yes, this would very likely identify the person.

It shouldn't be scary to use personal data, but the GDPR 'gurus' gave everyone a fright, so one of the most common things I hear when speaking to prospective clients is, "But can I even do email marketing with GDPR?" – and the answer is, "Of course, you just can't be a dick about it."

Personal data is data that identifies or could help identify a person. That's it. It's nothing spooky, you don't need a solicitor, and most people were already abiding by the principles of GDPR before it came into being.

How are you protecting it?

In a Newcastle office in 2007, a CD was sent in the post. It later transpired that it never reached its destination, and the identity and bank account details of some 25 million child benefit recipients were lost.

Unguarded by encryption and without the package being tracked, the CD was lost. Nobody really knows where it went, whether criminals got hold of it or whether it was just a balls up, but it's safe to say that someone most probably got sacked.

The incident almost toppled the then chancellor, Alistair Darling, and while it might seem that the data of your business is less important, in the post-GDPR world, people are a lot more conscious about what information they give out, and they expect it to be guarded properly.

There are two ways you can improve the data you keep: better passwords and increased security.

Most businesses will use some kind of platform like MailChimp, where the challenge is in keeping good passwords, which prevents the bad guys from waltzing in through the main gate.

If you're using Excel spreadsheets to hold all your customer data, your challenge is likely to be around improving data security and keeping the bad guys from scaling the walls of your castle.

Better passwords

You need good passwords. Ideally, they should be unique for every website you visit. NOT Smiles123, which you use for everything.

> A good way to check the effectiveness of your password is by going to https://password.kaspersky.com/ and testing it.

I typed in the password I used in the late 1990s and got:

⊗ A password change is long overdue!

- Bad news
  ⚠ Password is too short

- This password appeared 285 times in a database of leaked passwords.

Your password will be bruteforced with an average home computer in approximately...

9 seconds

Nine seconds to get hacked? Ouch.

"Nobody's going to hack my little business," I hear, but to brush off the basics of password hygiene is to fundamentally misunderstand how hacking works.

Let's say that a 'hacker' is a criminal wanting to get into a business and steal data, passwords and, ultimately, cash or an easy-to-change currency.

A common misconception is that a hacker sits down with the *Yellow Pages* and picks out the big companies.

The reality is a lot less exciting. One hacker creates lots of little programmes that attack every website they find. There's no specific pattern, it's just working through the internet trying to find businesses that aren't secure.

You don't have to be Fort Knox, but if you reuse the same password for your banking, email and the coffee reward app of your local café that just got hacked, you're putting everything at risk.

There is a long list of companies that went out of business because of a hack. Don't add yours to the list – assume a hacker's programme is always trying to break into your accounts. Make it harder with a strong password, or outsource the hard thinking to a password manager like 1Password or LastPass.

Now, each of my unique passwords would take quite a bit longer to get past:

> (✓) **Nice password!**
>
> • Your password is hack-resistant.
>
> • Your password does not appear in any databases of leaked passwords
>
> Your password will be bruteforced with an average home computer in approximately...
>
> **10000+ centuries**

There are other ways of using strong passwords:

» Use a master base key and then alter it with numbers or the website name.

» Use a sentence, which makes it exponentially more difficult to crack. (ILoveEmailsAndICannotLie! is rated at 10,000+ centuries, or uncrackable with today's technology.)

Increased security

If you're using an Excel sheet to hold customer data, it's really easy to keep it secure – put a password on it! That way, no matter if the file gets lost, stolen or damaged, the data inside is safe. (N.B. Do look after that password, though . . .)

Just remember to make it a good password, as I talked about in the previous section. This is the basics of how to secure the data you have about clients, customers and suppliers – basically, anyone you speak to in your business.

Most email platforms have a feature called Two Factor Authentication, which is a second layer of protection. If someone gets your password, they also need your phone, which will generate a random, six-digit number for you to type in – proving it's you.

This is super easy to set up. Download either the Google Authenticator or the Microsoft Authenticator app onto your phone. In MailChimp, this is in Account > Security > Enable Authenticator, and on other platforms it will live in the security or account settings page.

MailChimp then gives you a QR code to scan on the Authenticator app on your phone. You type in the six-digit number and you're all set. Next time you log in, once you've entered the username and password, you'll be prompted for the six-digit code in your app. It changes every 30 seconds and you'll be given the most up to date one.

It is a bit of a faff, I get it, but I always strongly recommend doing it, and MailChimp even give 10% off for enabling it, demonstrating how important they think it is, too.

So, now we've talked about protecting your clients' data, what kind of data do you want to collect?

What extra data do you collect?

Let's go back to Jess . . .

Jess has signed up and she's on the list!

What now?

You've now got a welcome sequence set up from the previous chapter, with some content examples. But I purposefully missed one out to talk about in more depth here.

Ask. More. Questions.

Poppy's Plants has a few different types of customers (we did this in the persona exercise further back), but when we've got just an email address, such as jess@gmail.com, how can we find out more information?

Turns out there's quite an easy answer: Ask them.

In my welcome sequence, I ask readers, "What's your biggest email marketing challenge?", and there are three options: "Getting set up and building a base", "Growing my list", or, "Converting readers into customers."

I'm asking for their pain point, so I can better help them scale up.

Depending on which option they pick, readers will see different sign-off lines and promotions, based on the product that's a better fit for where they are in their email marketing journey.

If they're just getting set up, it doesn't seem right to try and offer them an email audit, because they won't get the most out of it.

I also ask them what email platform they use – so I can make sure I don't send MailChimp course promotions to readers who don't use MailChimp.

Having the right data can lead you to making smarter decisions, and adding in a welcome survey to get more information from Jess once she's signed up can supercharge your automated personalisation.

How do I manage all my lists?

Have one master list/audience

It's common for businesses that have done some email marketing to have a bunch of lists in different pots all over the place. Normally, this comes from collecting email addresses from different places, such as from competitions, trade shows, business networking, in person and through organisations you are part of. Often, they can be kept as separate lists (either as Excel files on your computer, or as different lists in your email platform), but this often means you're not making the most of what email can offer.

The aim is to have one list and then tag people within it – creating segments (the email lingo for groups – not some special Terry's Chocolate Orange!).

A client job that still gives me nightmares some years on involved working with a charity that had over 17k readers, from over 40 different sources all over the place. My role was to come in and unify all of their lists, to make it easier for them to target the right people. It was messy and expensive.

It's so much easier if you start off by using one list from the very beginning. Not least because if you have a system, you can always tweak it to your evolving needs – and mostly so you don't have to end up hiring consultants to fix the problem!

This approach is easiest to start with and gives the greatest flexibility going forward.

The main objective of this type of set up is to give the strongest foundation. By having one master list, you can bring in email addresses from different places, such as from trade shows and from sign ups at networking events, etc.

The main strength in having one list is that it accurately captures the complete history of a reader. It doesn't matter if they interact with you by signing up on your homepage and then a few weeks later downloading a lead magnet – all that activity is merged, and you can see it in one place.

Separate lists = siloed data, and it's a lot less efficient. (They can't communicate with each other . . . so this makes your marketing much harder.)

USING MAILCHIMP: For MailChimp, when you get to a paid plan, this can actually end up costing you more, as you're billed by contact.

If a reader is in five different lists, they're counted as five separate contacts – so, if you have 10 lists containing the same email addresses for 1k people, you'd be billed for 10k email addresses.

As you plan for the future with your thousands of customers, you can see why getting it right early can help in the war on trying to get databases sorted.

Group/segment people to create many lists within one

In every email platform, there are ways to segment readers, and I'd strongly recommend using these segments instead of separate lists. I always advise sending the right communication (newsletters, products or reminders) to the right people (new customers, VIPs or readers who haven't purchased yet).

I'll be talking a lot more about segments and how to use them in the next chapter.

Trim regularly

Poppy's Plants is now gaining 100 new subscribers a week. That's great, but for some reason our open rate is going down.

This is weird, because our email sales are slightly up and we're getting so many new subscribers.

What could be going on?

Everybody will see dead wood in their list, as some readers don't engage as often. This shouldn't be seen as a terrible thing, to be avoided at all cost, it's a natural consequence of growth.

Once your list grows past your friends and family into people who have heard of you, and then to their degrees of connection, you'll end up with some dead wood.

The rule of thumb is: if a reader hasn't opened an email from you for 90 days, then get rid of them.

It helps them, as they won't be receiving emails they're not interested in, and it can help you by keeping your open rates high and keeping your email reputation strong.

There's another reason why it's good to cut out the dead wood, and it's that around 6% of email addresses a year stop working. And there's a few reasons for that:

1. They changed jobs and their work email address was deleted (especially for B2B email marketing).

2. They got married and created a new account with their new name.

3. They died.

REAL-WORLD EXAMPLE

I worked with a client using a very large and complex Customer Relationship Manager (CRM) tool, which powered emails, social adverts and direct mail posted out.

They had spent a lot of time and money on getting it just right, to help manage their tens of thousands of customers, but had overlooked a small detail – how to deal with customers who passed away.

A call centre operative, upon being informed a customer had died, for some unknown reason renamed a contact "Mr Dead".

Cut to three months later, and a widow received a sales catalogue addressed not to her late husband, but to "Mr Dead".

They got a new tick button in the CRM shortly afterwards to help automatically stop catalogues and emails going out. But not before an awful customer experience and some very bad PR.

Death is the most tragic reason, because while loved ones will probably check the email accounts of the deceased, they're not going to unsubscribe from every marketing email to help you out.

Have a process in place for dealing with people who pass away. Having a proactive plan will be helpful to their family who pick up the pieces.

So, every three months, make sure you take a look at who hasn't opened any emails since the last time you checked, and then unsubscribe them.

POWER UP

Supercharge Opt-outs

To supercharge automatic opt-outs, send out a last-chance saloon to see if you can persuade them to stay and start interacting with your reticent readers. If they do, fab – they're much more likely to start recognising your emails again and continue to engage. If not, they were probably only going to drag down your open rates anyway. And so, we let them go.

Win back

If you're going for gold, desperate to boost those open rates and get rid of the barnacles clinging to the hull of your HMS Email Marketing, let's talk about win-back sequences.

Almost every email platform will have a way to set this up.

It runs a daily check to see if anyone hasn't opened an email in the last 90 days, and if there are any new ones, it adds them to a new sequence.

Take a look at the example email over the page to see how you can implement this power up.

The most basic is just a single, simple reminder:

Subject line:	Do you still want to get plant emails?
Copy:	Hi Jess, I've noticed you haven't opened my weekly plant newsletter for a while now, and I just wanted to check if you still wanted to get them? If you do, all you have to do is click the big button that will take you to my blog. You'll keep getting the weekly plant newsletter. If you don't, I'll automatically unsubscribe you in a week. I want to help you get the most out of your houseplants, but I don't want to spam you if you're not finding it useful. No hard feelings and you can resubscribe at any time. If you've got any questions, don't hesitate to email me or phone on 0117 555 0123. Happy planting, Poppy
Button:	Confirm I want to get emails.

This has a friendly tone, and it's clear and concise.

This is a great example from Typeform:

Example 24 – Typeform's reminder sequence.

Once the reader opens and clicks the button, they'll be marked as active and fall back into your regular newsletter pot.

Otherwise, after a week, the email address will be automatically unsubscribed.

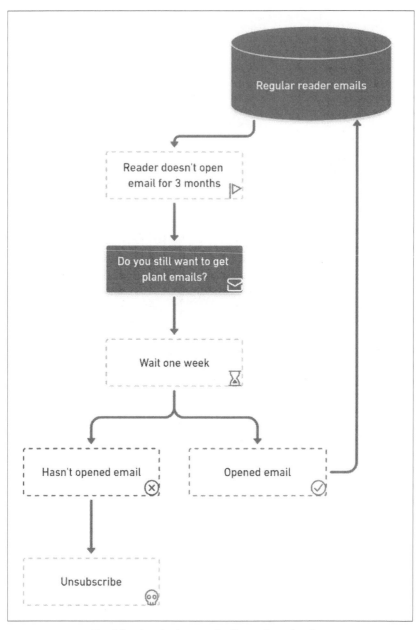

Email flowchart 2 – An example of how to 'sunset' readers.

Caveat – obviously, if you don't send out an email within 90 days, you could unintentionally unsubscribe everyone. But as you're following my advice, you're already emailing your list at least once a month.

If you're going to take an extended break from sending emails, always pause everything you've got going on to prevent mistakes like this from slipping through.

Collecting all the data you need can help you supercharge your email marketing to the next level, making it work smarter, not harder. Now that we've covered getting data, let's look at what to do with it.

Chapter 8: Working Smarter

Let's use the data you've just collected to subtly nudge readers into becoming customers.

Anything that helps you to put the right message in front of the right person at the right time is going to have a really positive impact on clicks, sales and revenue.

I often speak to potential clients who are using the same spray-and-pray scattergun method that was popular twenty years ago. But these days, a personalised campaign that resonates with readers is what really brings in the results.

I said this before in Section One – Chapter 2: *Planning Emails*, but any objective that has a target audience of 'everyone' really means 'nobody'. It must be targeted, otherwise it will get lost in the background noise of every other email programme doing the same.

To make your emails stand out, get personal. And all that data you've just collected in the last chapter will help you do just that.

Segmentation

Simply put, a segment is a bunch of readers that are grouped together because of:

>   » Something you **KNOW** about them (like they have a garden, or that they live in a house).

>   » Something they have (or haven't) **DONE** (like purchasing an indoor plant or downloading a plant-care guide).

There are a million different ways to set this up, and the email platforms give you so many possibilities that it's hard to know where to even start.

Looking at a blank screen can make it difficult to get going, so let's see how Poppy's Plants is getting on with segmentation and work through a couple of example segments that would help (that you might want to copy).

Poppy's Plants KNOWS a few things about its readers (other than their email address!):

» Their first name

» Whether they live in a flat or a house

» If they have a garden

» Their birthday

Poppy's Plants can also see a few things that readers have (or haven't) DONE:

» Made a purchase

» Downloaded an eBook

» Opened an email

» Clicked an email

Poppy's Plants sends out a weekly Plant Tips newsletter, with the aim of educating readers about plant care, as well as increasing sales.

It features a plant of the week, one of ten eBooks, some shop news and a funny story. Readers like Poppy's honest personality, and her knowledge flows through her prose.

Now, the first place to start is to look at what data we can use. Let's look at Jess, the budding *(not even sorry for that one!)* plant parent.

Jess has said that she lives in a flat and doesn't have a garden. She's already downloaded our 'Getting started with indoor plants guide'. From this, it can be assumed that Jess is likely to be a beginner and that something simple, like a spider plant, might be suitable for her.

When the newsletter is built, blocks can be set so it's only seen by certain types of people. How this works is different for each email platform, so ask yours how to get this working. It's likely to be called conditional content or personalisation blocks.

If you're using MailChimp, I go through this in detail in my Chimp Hero MailChimp course, in the data and e-commerce section. Available from chimphero.com, use BETTEREMAILS for 15% off.

eBooks and ratcheting up the content tree

The main idea is not to prompt readers towards a free eBook that they've already downloaded. For example, Poppy's Plants might want to promote the indoor plant guide to everyone to start off with, but then prompt readers to download more advanced guides:

→ Show 'Getting started with indoor plants guide' to everyone, except those who have already downloaded it.

→ Show 'Indoor plant watering schedule print out' to readers who have downloaded the indoor plant guide above.

→ Show 'The indoor plants that love your bathroom' to readers who have downloaded the watering schedule above.

→ Show 'Challenge yourself with these tricky plants' to readers who have downloaded the indoor plants for the bathroom guide above.

The main idea is similar to the previous example, but it uses something the reader has **DONE** rather than what is **KNOWN** about them.

This can seem like a bit of a faff to get going, but if you set it up once, it'll mean you're not prompting someone to download an eBook they've already got.

It can be a really good way of maximising engagement and minimising redundant call-to-actions (because they've already taken them).

Have you ever seen an online advert just after you've bought a product? With digital marketing (and email in particular) there's no need to waste advertising. Keep on task and focus on getting readers to engage more through things they haven't seen before – they'll ignore it otherwise.

POWER UP

Setting these up as segments in your email platform can also be a great way to go the extra mile by sending a follow-up email a few days after the reader downloads, to check they got the link and to prompt any questions.

This can be as simple as, "Reply to this email if you need a hand picking out the perfect plant for your place."

Or go even further, giving related blog posts on your site and related products from the eBook.

Have a think about the data you currently collect or are planning to get. How might you group readers into their tribes for a better experience?

If you're wondering if there are segments that better fit your business, book in a Power Hour, where we can talk through your situation and I can recommend the best approach. Head over to sendbetter.email/powerhour if you want to go through a few scenarios that would make sense for your business.

Personalisation

So, now you've got a few ideas on how to group and segment your readers, how should you address them?

"Hi Jon" is a great first step to getting personalisation up and running.

But if you don't know the reader's first name, what should you call them?

"Hi First Name" doesn't look great and leaving it blank looks weird.

Always think of a fallback that's appropriate for you and your brand.

For Emails Explained, my email marketing newsletter from Inbox Hero, if I don't know the reader's first name, I'll call them "Inbox Apprentice".

At Poppy's Plants, it's "Plant Parent".

I've seen other examples where it's "friend" or "member". All this is done to try and make it feel less jarring for the recipient when their name isn't known.

You could use roles like "business owner", or just keep it nice and simple with "reader".

This is one of the nice little touches that takes a few seconds to set up and helps to avoid awkward blank spaces.

But personalisation goes a lot deeper than just adding the reader's name or a friendly title into the email. It's also about making sure the email drops in at the right moment.

For example, a garage that does annual vehicle MOT tests might have a campaign that reminds customers eleven months after their last test that it's about to expire. That's a personal experience to the reader and a useful nudge that in their world they need to do something (like book an MOT!).

I really loved the mid-2010s British Gas adverts featuring customers in their houses on individual planets, with the line, "Looking after your world." Personalisation is the key to making those readers feel like you care about them and their world.

The best personalisation is invisible.

The absolute best examples of this, and I'm talking email marketing on steroids at huge companies, is where weather data is being used, which involves displaying different images depending on the reader's location: a rainy image if they are somewhere wet, snow if it's very cold and an image with a summery feel if there's a heatwave.

I've seen some really successful email campaigns by outdoor sport companies, where they offer durable tents if it's pouring down near you, or display a range of sunglasses if the mercury heads over 25°C.

The reader has no idea, but because it connects with their local surroundings it feels more personal, like the email understands them. This kind of invisible profiling is super effective.

CASE STUDY #2: Middletons Mobility

Let's go a bit deeper, with a look into how a mobility firm I worked with got the invisible personalisation that supercharged their welcome and newsletter programmes.

The example I've chosen is from quite a big project, but you can use it as inspiration for how you could add some behind-the-scenes magic to surprise and delight your readers.

Middletons Mobility is a retail chain of adjustable beds, chairs and mobility scooters, with stores in over 20 cities.

One of the main calls-to-action on the website was to request a brochure. The overriding purpose of this was to encourage prospects into the store, where the products could be demonstrated on a racetrack outside, to help would-be customers get a feel for the equipment.

The main challenge the company faced with its email marketing was to support this push to get readers into stores.

From the details the visitor had entered on the website, Middletons knew where they lived (from the postcode) and what product they were interested in (a chair, a bed or a scooter), because of the web page they had visited.

From this, the reader's postcode could be used to provide them with the details of their nearest store. This worked in exactly the same way as the Poppy's Plants example, where Jess was prompted to say whether she had a garden or not.

The behind-the-scenes personalisation blocks look at each reader and make a decision: "You're Bristol, so you'll see the Bristol showroom card."

Discover our Middletons Bristol Showroom

Middletons Bristol was the world's first Middletons store. It's one of most beautiful flagship showrooms and has been much-loved by customers since it opened in 2013.

VIEW THE BRISTOL SHOWROOM

Case study example 1 – Bristol showroom location card.

"This reader has a CF postcode, so their nearest store is Cardiff:"

Case study example 2 – Cardiff showroom location card.

This, combined with seasonal offer blocks that were dotted around welcome sequences and newsletters, meant there were hundreds of different variations of emails going out, all automatically.

It's the invisible personalisation, like only promoting the category of product they've looked at, that really helps readers feel like you care, without the creepy, "We're watching you!" vibe.

Case study example 3 – Main image for a customer who had requested a chair brochure.

This example, from one of the first emails that visitors received from Middletons, is tailored depending on which brochure they asked for.

This is the image that people who requested a chair brochure saw, and there were different versions for the beds and scooters.

The customer probably wouldn't even notice this was being personalised, but would, perhaps subconsciously, think, "That's the product I was interested in! I was just looking at that a little while ago."

Case study example 4 – An advert banner for a reader who had requested a chair brochure.

And then, right at the bottom of the email, Middletons had another advert block highlighting the product category again and providing several options to get back to the same information. All this was to encourage a purchase, and it all worked exceptionally well, boosting open rates, click rates and, ultimately, store visits and purchases.

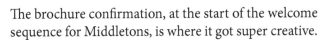

Power up:

Supercharging the first email touchpoint

The brochure confirmation, at the start of the welcome sequence for Middletons, is where it got super creative.

As the reader had requested a brochure, they got an email shortly afterwards saying, "Your brochure should be with you shortly."

But the visual included a little image personalisation, showing a brochure hitting a welcome mat. The address the brochure was being posted out to was also added to the email.

Here's an example from our imaginary reader, Jess:

Example 25 – Image personalisation bringing in customer data.

It visually shows what's about to happen and backs up what's being said (in the text) in the rest of the email.

The best thing about this kind of image personalisation?

It's a lot easier to get going with than you might think.

Image personalisation

After seeing some examples of big companies sending out images with text baked into them, you might be wondering, "How on earth do they do it?!"

This has traditionally only been available to companies with large budgets, but not anymore.

I've got a great recommendation: **NiftyImages.com** – it's free for small senders, so if you're starting out, you can use it for up to 10k email opens, without paying a penny.

It's a good tool for beginners to the personalised image world, and the super-intuitive website makes it easy. They've also got some great pre-built templates – like this one I made and included in my Christmas e-card:

Example 26 – Merry Christmas, Jess.

You can upload any image and then add on any kind of text, which you can then include in your email. It'll ask you what email platform you use, and you'll need to dig around it for the field names, but it's pretty straightforward.

Have a look at some super simple but really striking examples from leading UK brands:

Example 27 – Chocolates for Jess.

Example 28 – A coffee for Jess.

I wouldn't recommend using this in every email you send, but where it makes sense it can add that little touch of, "Oh! That's nice."

How to set up image personalisation

→ Create an image with some blank space for text.

→ Upload that picture to Nifty Images.

→ Add the text and customise the size, colour and font (you can also add a fallback if there isn't any text).

→ Nifty Images will give you the code to use in your email platform.

For Poppy's Plants, this might be a loyalty card programme, as part of the newsletter, which includes a mock-up of their loyalty card:

Example 29 – An example reward card image that's been personalised.

Image personalisation won't be at the top of your to-do list, but once you're well settled into an email rhythm and you're comfortable, try and visualise how it might fit your business.

And then do it.

If you're struggling for some inspiration or you're thinking, "This will never work for me!" then let's put some time in the diary to chat through where you are, and I can give you some ideas on how you might make the most of it. Head to sendbetter.email/powerhour.

Data-led automated emails

Birthday emails

If you've got a loyalty programme or collect readers' birthdays, you can get a birthday email campaign set up really quickly.

Birthday emails are the easiest campaigns to set up. They're engaged with the most and reflect a personal experience that everyone shares.

The best examples are those that 'surprise and delight', normally through offering a free, low-value product such as a coffee or cookie.

This one comes from Subway, because who doesn't want a free cookie on their birthday?!

Example 30 – Subway's birthday email.

Another great one is from Greggs. It has a simpler tone and is backed up with the reward being redeemed in the recipient's mobile app:

:: GREGGS

Happy Birthday, Jon - Have a free treat!

We've added a free treat to your rewards. Choose a sweet treat at Greggs and enjoy it on us! To find out more about how to claim your free treat - and for full terms and conditions of this offer - go to the My Rewards page in the app.

Enjoy,

Greggs

Example 31 – The Greggs birthday email.

And for fans of the fizz, the Pizza Express chain offer readers a free bottle of bubbly when they book a table for their birthday. It's quite a long, thin email, which makes it perfect for mobile – and the animated dough balls pulling on the balloon string make for a very playful theme:

Example 32 – Happy birthday from Pizza Express.

All of these are amazing demonstrations of the 'surprise and delight' principle, which focuses on the idea that readers who get a reward out of the blue tend to think much more positively about the business. This increases Customer Lifetime Value, as well as making for great personal moments, when readers get something for nothing.

I'd recommend giving away a small thing completely free, rather than a discount, because it shows the business cares about the customer beyond the immediate sales cycle. Additionally, in most of these examples, when readers go to redeem the voucher, they're very likely to add more items to their basket – so it really does pay to be nice!

I've got loads more examples and screenshots (including a great half-birthday email!) in my Birthday Email Guide, which is available at sendbetter.email/birthday. Use the code BETTEREMAILS to get it free (as it's normally sold for £9.97).

POWER UP

Advanced automations

If your business has a lot of user-generated content (like social media sites), or you're always collecting data about your users based on what they do (like mobile or web apps), then data-led automation emails can give you the edge.

The best example of this that you might have seen is the Spotify Wrapped Year-in-Review of listeners' song choices. This campaign is supported by a ton of PR and billboards, and it separates user data into fun tidbits.

"Dear 3,749 people who streamed 'It's the End of the World As We Know It' the day of the Brexit vote, hang in there."

"Dear person who played 'Sorry' 42 times on Valentine's Day. What did you do?"

These types of emails pull in data that Spotify has about the individual user's listening habits and highlights the top artists the user has listened to and the most played songs.

A lot of this section is going to focus on how apps use email marketing by using the vast amount of data they have about readers.

This is most suitable for businesses that collect lots of data, or data about how their customers use their service. It might not be relevant for your situation, but do have a look through this case study and see if anything rings a bell. Then think about what you might be able to adapt for your business.

CASE STUDY #3: MySunshine app

MySunshine is a mobile and web app that's the brainchild of Kieran Fitzsimons. It helps new parents securely store, share and cherish the memories of their babies and children as they grow. From helpfully adding how old children are when the photos and videos are taken, to being able to control who can see what, it's an easy-to-use app to keep as an online memory book.

This was a great project to work on, as it involved starting from zero. It was a blank canvas that had several layers to it: what needs to be done NOW, what should be done SOON and what would be great to do SOME DAY. Splitting out ideas into these categories helped prioritisation.

I worked with Kieran before the app's public launch to look at how email could help with the three key challenges he faced:

» Onboarding new users (crucial for apps!).

» Encouraging upgrades to the premium plan.

» Retaining those premium users.

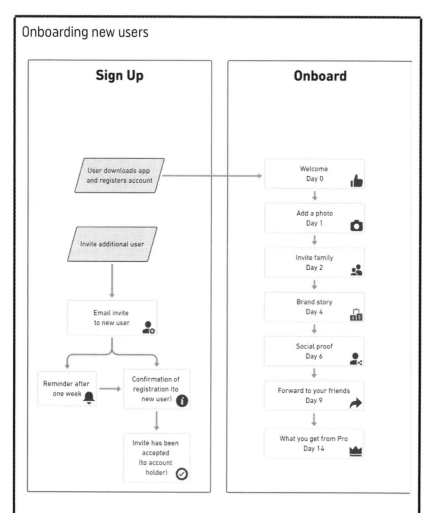

Case study flowchart 1 – The initial stages of welcoming new sign ups.

The biggest challenge for apps is getting people used to all the features, so they create habits and keep coming back. The moment a user signs up, they're added into a drip sequence that will familiarise them with all the features and benefits.

Upgrading to premium

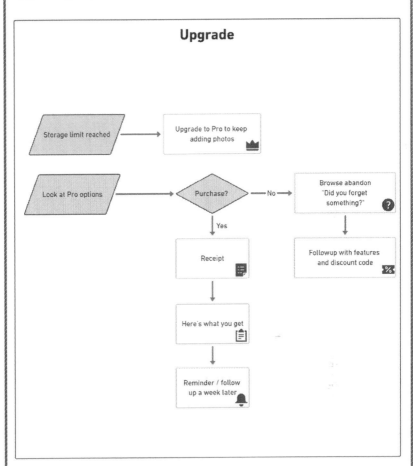

Case study flowchart 2 – An upgrade sequence.

These two sequences look at when a user approaches or reaches the limit for the free plan, with an upgrade email. Same for if a free users goes onto the view pricing page, they'd get a "Were you interested in our Premium?" email. These kinds of subtle nudges can be powerful for readers sitting on the fence.

Retaining premium users

Renew

Renewal in 14 days

Is card still valid? —No→ Update your card / payment details

Yes

Your account is about to renew ℹ️

Renewal successful? —Yes→ Thanks for staying with us ✓

No

You're about to lose your Pro features ⚠️

Your account has been cancelled
+ 3 days ⊗

Renew your Pro subscription (discount)
+ 7 days ↻

Case study flowchart 3 – A renewal sequence.

It was a real pleasure to work on this project, which focused on the whole user experience lifecycle, from sign up to upgrade, renewal and sunset (where a user no longer actively uses the app). Kieran also gave me a great testimonial:

"Jon immediately identified what we were doing and hadn't considered, then built and presented a thorough plan to us on how to improve our email campaigns. He covered everything from user onboarding to client retention and referrals, lots of which we had not even thought about! I would highly recommend Inbox Hero, no matter which email platform your company uses."

Kieran Fitzsimons, CEO, MySunshine

If you're wondering where to start, have a look through the Putting it All Together chapter and then let's get a Power Hour booked in. Head to sendbetter.email/powerhour.

Chapter 9: What's next?

Once you've got readers signed up, opening your emails and buying something . . . what's next? This is probably one of the most neglected parts of any customer experience, and it's not just confined to email. The post-purchase experience can leave customers feeling a bit confused, especially if they've just spent money on a personalised service or a high-ticket item with no update or follow-up.

Depending on your product or service, you might want to capture feedback, remind buyers how to use what they've bought and keep them interested with new products. If products are consumable (like pet food), this could even involve reminders on when to stock up again based on the order.

A high number of online retailers will go for the big pitch, get the sale and then the customer will get a receipt and nothing else.

Making sure there's a good deal of focus on what happens after someone purchases, in that gap between inputting their credit card details through to the next few days and weeks until delivery, can help to solidify why they bought from you, thus improving their long-term customer lifetime value.

In this section, we'll look at the different types of post-purchase emails, with a view to getting you to identify which would work for your business.

Getting the sequence right

It looks like a lot of emails, but not all of them will work for what you do. Read on to find out more, before focusing on the few that will fit best with your business:

» Abandoned basket

» Receipt

» Delivery notification/gap

» Reviews

» Follow up

» Care/usage instructions

» Cross-sells and upsells

» Replenishment reminder

» Refer a friend

» Loyalty scheme/VIP membership club

» Onboarding

» Non-recent customers

Abandoned basket

Just before we look at all the post-purchase emails, let's recap a really easy win for businesses selling online: the abandoned basket.

You might have already heard the term before, it's sometimes also called abandoned cart, but it's where a website visitor adds an item to their basket, goes to the checkout and gets nearly to the end, but, for whatever reason, doesn't buy.

There are a variety of reasons why, like the example we had of Jess on the bus earlier getting interrupted mid email, or, if checkouts ask for a lot of information it increases the chance a visitor might get interrupted.

Unforeseen extras can be another common reason why visitors leave, for example, tax or postage charges. If Jess was going to buy a £30 orchid, only to find out the sales tax (VAT) wasn't added, and then the postage was expensive, at the moment of being asked for her card number it could be that she realises she's being asked to pay quite a bit more than she originally thought and decides to leave.

Then there are the window shoppers. They want to know the price and get halfway through the buying process, but then hum and haw to themselves before eventually talking themselves out of the purchase.

Once set up, the abandoned basket automatically emails website visitors that almost completed (so long as they got as far as entering their email address!) with a reminder.

Here's a great example from Lego:

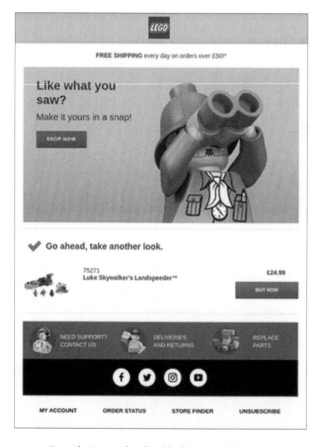

Example 33 – An abandoned basket example from Lego.

It's fairly common to include a discount code to push people off the fence. A 10% discount can double the number of abandoned baskets that are revived, but obviously that price comes off your bottom line – it can be a very tricky balancing act.

USING MAILCHIMP: If you're using WordPress (free) with the WooCommerce e-commerce plugin (free), then MailChimp can set this up automatically for you.

Connect your website to your MailChimp account and then create a new automated email.

You'll see an option for an abandoned cart template that you can modify. Once you click publish, it'll send out abandoned basket emails automatically, just like magic.

> I recommend using the MailChimp, WordPress and WooCommerce trifecta, and I go into more detail concerning how to set this up in the last chapter, Putting it All Together. You can also join my ChimpHero.com course, where I walk students through how to set it up step-by-step.

Test it every three months to make sure it's working as you'd expect, and that everything is all still ticking over.

I recall when I used 99 Designs (a graphic design service) for a logo for my Email Examples project. I went through the checkout process, paid and got a receipt. About an hour later, I received a, "You left something behind" email, with all the details of the project I'd just paid for.

Sometimes, there are just tech gremlins, so I suggest a "P.S. If you've just purchased, please ignore and accept our apologies" line at the end to reassure those who have just purchased that it did in fact go through – otherwise, in the worst-case scenario, they might try and make the same purchase again and get two items.

What's the post-purchase experience?

Before we get into post-purchase email sequences, let's take a minute to think about the post-purchase experience as a whole.

First and foremost, it's dominated by how the customer feels. Customers are humans, and they have emotions, opinions and feelings. Making sure they feel confident in their purchase, that they're informed about the progress and gently reminded to restock or maintain a product will decrease buyer's remorse and increase return custom.

Here is the best way to find out what type of sequence to follow up with after purchase.

> There's a blank version of this for you to print out at sendbetter.email/resources, or you can get a plain piece of paper and sketch it out.

→ *Who is your typical customer? (We covered this earlier in Section One – Chapter 2: Planning Emails.)*

→ *Where do customers typically hear about you?*

→ *How do customers typically interact with your content? (Social media, email, blogs?)*

→ *What typically prompts customers into making a purchase? (A newsletter, advert, promotion?)*

→ *What product are customers typically buying? (Orchids are a bestseller at Poppy's Plants.)*

→ *How do they normally buy? (Telephone, in person, online, card, PayPal, cash?)*

Reader Persona

Who is your reader?	What else are they doing just before/after reading your emails?	Where do they read your emails?	How long have they got when they read your emails?	Demographics

What other emails do they receive?				

Why do/did they sign up? (The need)	What value do your emails add? (The solution)

When (day and time) is best for them to read your emails?	What device are they reading your email on?

Who isn't your reader? (Who do you want to repel from signing up)	

An example Reader Persona template that you can download and fill in.

Now that we've mapped out how customers got to purchasing, there are a few more questions to keep the thinking going regarding how your business works today. We'll be looking at each of these in detail as we go through this chapter, so be sure to read to the end before skipping to the bit you want to focus on the most:

→ *Is there a wait between purchase and delivery? (Normally that's a yes for e-commerce and services.)*

→ *If yes, what expectations are set? (Normally a delivery date or details of next steps.)*

→ *Do you follow up with customers to check they're happy?*

→ *Do you ask customers to review you?*

→ *Do you ask customers to fill in a survey or give feedback?*

→ *Do you ask customers to sign up for a newsletter or to follow social media accounts?*

→ *Do you show customers other services or products they might be interested in?*

→ *Are there any specific times of year that the customer ought to do something with your product? (Like bringing your plant indoors as it transitions to autumn, or putting your bulbs in a cool, dark place for the winter.)*

Let's have a look at a few examples through the Poppy's Plants' lens.

Jess has been getting the Plant Parent newsletter for a while and after seeing an article on how to care for orchids, she's going to give it a go. She buys an orchid starter kit that comes with an orchid, pot and enough feed for three months.

Poppy's Plants sends some items recorded delivery because they're valuable or heavy, but smaller plants are sent in the regular mail, so the delivery date is not always known.

There are a few things that Poppy's Plants can do to set Jess's expectations and help her to make the most out of the purchase:

» **Immediately:** Receipt and delivery/collection instructions.

» **A day later:** Picking out a spot for your orchid. (Sunny, warm, best places – link to article.)

» **After delivery (or a week after order):** How to get the most out of your orchid.

» **Two weeks after delivery (or three weeks after order):** Was everything OK with your delivery? Review us on this platform and help our business grow.

» **Two and a half months after order:** Re-order some orchid feed soon.

It's easier to look at this in a flowchart:

Email flowchart 3 – An example post-purchase sequence.

Let's take a look at the different types of post-purchase emails there are. Not all of them will be applicable to your business, but whether you're a service business, retail or e-commerce, at least a few will be useful and can kickstart your thinking on building a better post-buying experience.

The first few we'll go through are more focused towards buying products, the next towards all businesses, and then we'll finish up with emails that are best for membership or subscription businesses.

Receipt

The classic, humble receipt is often overlooked, but it will often be the most opened email ever – it's typical to see 80% to 90% open rates for these types of emails.

And that's why it's super important to make sure that:

→ All the information is right. (You'd be surprised at the number of receipts I've seen with the wrong dates or currency!)

→ There's a clear "What next" action.

→ There are some other products the reader might be interested in.

Take a look at a great example from Audible over the page.

We can see what we've ordered, there's a clear "Start listening" action to take and then at the bottom, "You might like these listens", which cross-sells a related item (we'll talk more about that in a little while).

The main aim of receipts is to recap the order and communicate what's to come, but they can include more information, and as they're so well opened, it gives you an opportunity to communicate more than just the price.

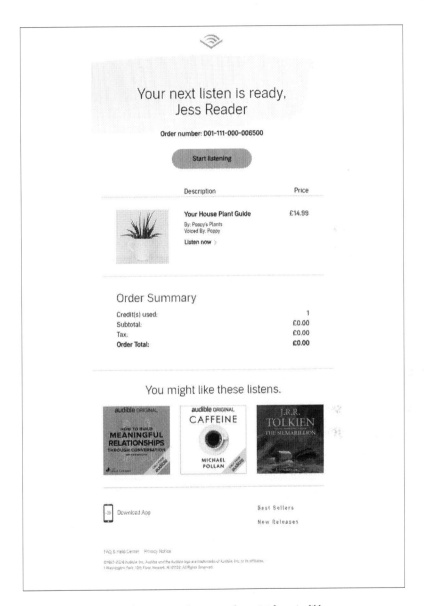

Example 34 – A purchase example receipt from Audible.

Let's look at this example from Uber in the US*:

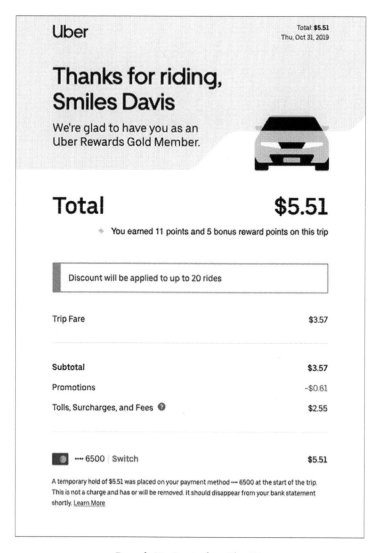

Example 35 – Receipt from Uber US.

It does what it needs to – highlights the trip taken – and is set out in a typical receipt format. If you view the whole email at sendbetter.email/uber, you'll see that it also includes a benefit that all rideshare trips are insured to give the reader peace of mind. Towards the bottom, there's a refer-a-friend share code and an option to learn more about Uber's currency, which is ideal for driving up loyalty and customer lifetime value.

Another great example of helping the reader understand what's next comes from Chipotle, a Mexican restaurant chain in the US*:

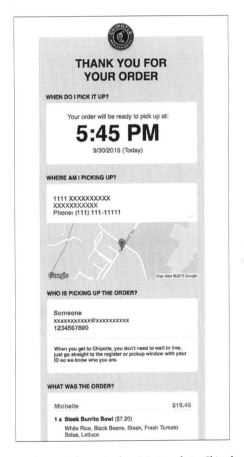

Example 36 – Order receipt from Mexican chain, Chipotle.

This receipt is broken up into questions:

→ *When do I pick it up?*

→ *Where am I picking up?*

→ *Who is picking up the order?*

→ *What was the order?*

It's a really simple but effective email. And as the reader is rushing to their local branch to pick up the order, this question and answer-based format makes it that little bit easier for them to process all the information.

Receipts are more than just an automated email with numbers on. They help readers to understand their purchase and they answer their immediate questions. Have a think about what else you might want to include in your receipt template. Don't overdo it, though, receipts should be simple, and I'd suggest focusing your efforts on tweaking what you've already got rather than reinventing the wheel.

AND WHAT'S THE BEST E-MAIL ADDRESS TO REWARD YOUR LOYALTY WITH AN ENDLESS BARRAGE OF SPAM?

© marketoonist.com

I have a short, cautionary tale before we move on: Don't mistake a purchase for, "Now sign me up to the newsletter and spam me." I became a victim of this when purchasing a shirt at a well-known retailer. At the checkout, I was asked if I wanted an email copy of the receipt instead and said sure thing, only to find that in addition to the receipt, I got signed up to the promotional newsletter. The cartoon on the previous page sums it up beautifully!

Most suitable for: Businesses who take any form of payment online or in store.

The delivery notification/gap

If you're sending physical items in the post, there will be a gap between the purchase and the delivery. This time can be really critical, especially if you sell memberships or a complex product that requires some setup or additional work.

Here are a couple of great examples. First from the meal kit company HelloFresh (see Example 37 over the page) after a customer purchases their inaugural box but before it's delivered, and second from the virtual bank Monzo (see Example 38, also over the page), before a customer receives their card in the post.

HelloFresh's approach sets the reader up for success, by introducing them to four main things they want them to know before their first meal box arrives:

- » How to choose recipes
- » Go to recipes to find basic ingredients
- » How to skip a week
- » Download the app

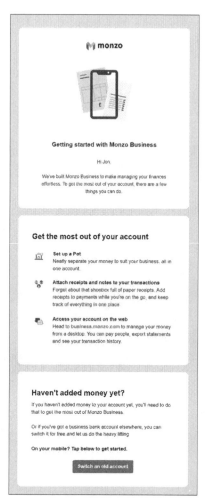

Example 37 & 38 – Confirmation and next steps from HelloFresh & Monzo business account setup confirmation email.

I've worked with quite a collection of subscription and software businesses, and the reason this kind of email is so important is that it reduces churn (the amount of people who cancel between regular payments). This kind of welcome can reduce churn by a couple of per cent, thus saving money you would have otherwise lost to a cancellation.

It's designed to be as helpful as possible and is an effort to train the customer into making the most out of their product/service, so that they remain loyal. Especially for a weekly meal box delivery, it's important that customers know how to pick their favourite meals and be able to skip a week if they're on holiday. This will save them being greeted by a box of rotten food on their doorstep when they get back.

This is the first in a few post-purchase emails that are traditionally called 'onboarding', and they are often found in subscriptions and memberships (usually physical subscription boxes or digital software), where payments are regularly made. I've included some more examples of these, and a template for Poppy's Plants, in a dedicated onboarding section of this chapter.

The second example (on the previous page) comes from Monzo, the app-based bank. It's the email it sends to business customers after they've set up an account but before getting their card. It focuses on 'Get the most out of your account' and features a prompt to move bank accounts under the Account Switch scheme. Bank accounts are complex beasts, and getting users to start using a new one regularly is the difference between an active user and a customer who tries it and never logs back in again.

Most suitable for: Businesses that have a gap between purchase and delivery (physical or virtual).

It's on the way (Dispatch notification)

A receipt is sent immediately after the order, but the 'dispatched' email is the one sent after the item has been packaged up and has left the warehouse to go to the courier for delivery. It can help customers understand when their order is likely to arrive and, if tracked, there will often be a 'track your order' link.

But, like the receipt, you can always add a few flourishes.

This example from Lakeland is clear in that the order has gone from the warehouse to the courier and it'll be delivered soon. But it also prompts the user to sign up for the newsletter, as well as giving customer service information. There is a big block at the bottom about *The Lakeland Guarantee*, which will make readers feel a lot more confident in their purchase, even before it arrives, that it's guaranteed for three years:

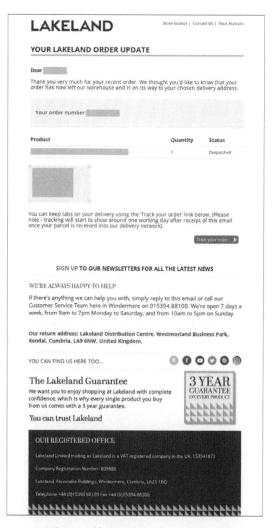

Example 39 – Adding marketing in a receipt email

I could go on and show you loads of examples, but the key thing to take away from this is that it helps the reader understand where their order is and improves their confidence that they've made the right decision in buying your product or service. To hear silence from a company and be left not knowing if/when the item will be delivered can be a bit unnerving, especially if it's something with an emotional connection, has a high value or has been hyped up.

Most suitable for: Businesses sending any physical items in the mail.

Shipment check-in

Delivery check-in emails normally come from the courier and give a tracking link.

This example from the meal kit company HelloFresh, through the courier DPD, shows a fairly standard delivery notification, letting the reader know the order has been successfully delivered:

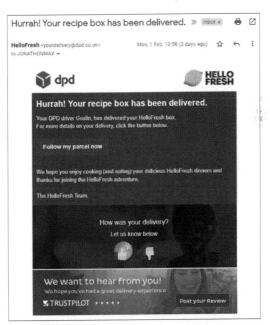

Example 40 – A delivery notification.

It comes from a DPD email address, but also features the HelloFresh logo. As well as letting the reader know their box has been delivered, it tells them that more details can be found on the tracking link. It's worded from the HelloFresh team and wishes the customer an enjoyable experience cooking and eating their meal kits.

It also allows for the reader to leave feedback about the courier with a simple thumbs up or down, which would most likely be passed onto an internal team to track driver performance.

In addition, there's a prompt to rate DPD on Trustpilot. This type of social validation can really help online businesses, and we'll cover asking for reviews in just a second.

Delivery notifications tend to be shorter and simpler, but if you can add in your own brand, it can help the reader know which parcel the courier is talking about (especially if they are a prolific online shopper!), and it can be a good way to highlight any problems with deliveries straight away. Again, as with the receipt, err on the side of being more basic – nobody has time for a *War and Peace* length essay about their order update.

Most suitable for: Businesses sending physical items in the mail, especially those that are tracked or signed for high value (£250+) parcels.

Review/feedback

Asking for a review or feedback is super helpful for businesses. It validates they do a good job and that their previous customers have been happy. This gives the new or potential customer peace of mind that they're not being swindled by a rip-off merchant.

Speaking of reviews, have you reviewed this book yet? If you've found it useful so far, I'd be eternally grateful for a review on Amazon. You can do that by going to sendbetter.email/review. I'd also love to hear from you direct about what you think of the book, and I would be happy to answer any questions you might have at jon@inboxhero.co.uk.

If you've got an online store, this can be set up automatically, and it's really easy if you use a platform like Trustpilot[1]. It can connect with your online store and sort it all out for you (even on the free Trustpilot plan).

As for the customer, they're certainly not thinking, "OMG, I must remember to write a five-star review for that thing I bought!" – it's not even on their to-do list. So, a gentle reminder a reasonable time after the order can really help to boost the number of reviews.

A study from Econsultancy showed that reviews produce an average 18% uplift in sales and are trusted 12 times more than the product description from a manufacturer.[2]

There can be a number of SEO benefits, but as I'm an email man, I'll stay in my lane and stick to saying it's good for your website. Prompting for reviews through email is one of the biggest drivers for getting them.

But take note: it requires a bit more prompting to get people who are happy with a product to leave a review than it does those who are unhappy. This is to do with loss aversion theory, the idea that a person who sees £100 go down the drain will lose more satisfaction than the satisfaction they would gain from winning £100.

Some companies offer a coupon for a future purchase in exchange for writing a review. That gives an incentive for the customer, and it also gets them thinking about their next purchase. This great win-win idea has helped brands like Seriously Silly Socks boost their sales by 60%.[3]

Or, if you make it really easy for the customer, such as only asking them to rate you by a star method, it'll take them less time to leave a review, thus making it more likely that they'll go ahead with it.

Reviews don't necessarily have to be traditional ones. If you're a personal brand business, such as a consultant, you might instead ask for a LinkedIn recommendation. I use LinkedIn and regularly ask clients to leave feedback there, as it's more appropriate for B2B-type businesses.

Most suitable for: Almost all businesses.

1. Trustpilot (n.d.) Research finding. https://uk.business.trustpilot.com/marketing/trust-mark-research
2. Charlton, C. (2012). *Ecommerce consumer reviews: why you need them and how to use them.* https://econsultancy.com/ecommerce-consumer-reviews-why-you-need-them-and-how-to-use-them/
3. Cotton, B. (2019). Retail brands killing it with great reviews. *Business Leader.* https://www.businessleader.co.uk/retail-brands-killing-it-with-great-reviews/66100/

Follow up (Did everything arrive OK?)

At the beginning of this jigsaw piece, we saw the example from Poppy's Plants of a follow up to make sure everything arrived in order.

This kind of email helps weed out any smaller issues that the customer may not have wanted to bring up, but it can also turn up interesting feedback you might not have otherwise heard, which you can then act upon.

If you're thinking about sending an email to request a review, get this one out first and you'll have the opportunity to resolve a few of the smaller complaints before they go on a public review site.

Most suitable for: Businesses sending perishable or fragile products, or complex services that require several steps to get working.

Should be paired with: The review/feedback email.

Care/usage instructions

Selling a pair of sunglasses? It should(!) be fairly straightforward, and I don't think you need a "How to use" email.

Selling a plant? It might be an idea to send an email to remind the customer how to look after it, even if those instructions are also in the box. If I've learned anything doing emails for as long as I have, it's that customers absorb information differently. Some will read the email from top to bottom and others will glance through it at warp speed, but if the customer has a problem, it's likely they'll come back to the email to try and resolve it.

These emails also work great for software or apps. The example over the page from Amazon Web Services provides a clear way forward, with a step-by-step guide on what's next. It actually conveys a lot of information and links, but presenting it in a nice, four-stage approach means it's simple without being basic.

Example 41 – Simple, clear and numbered call-to-actions help guide the eye.

Here's another example from the energy provider Bulb, to customers who get a smart meter.

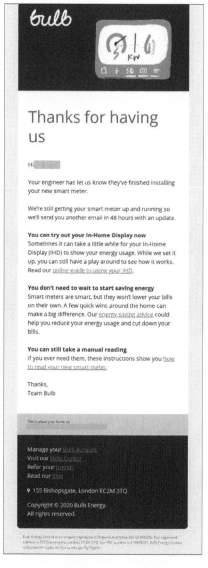

Example 42 – Following up from a smart meter installation.

Smart meters are a different way of reading gas and electric meters, so these types of 'how to' instructions can be really helpful in reducing calls into the contact centre, as well as customer frustration in something not working as expected.

These links can be used in the coming months and years in case the physical manual is lost. It also does a great job of telling the reader what's next, with, "We'll send you another email in 48 hours with an update." This helps to set expectations regarding what's coming:

Most suitable for: Businesses selling products or services that need maintenance.

Cross-sells and upsells (You might like...)

We touched on cross-sells and upsells as a useful way to boost the average order value, but let's go a bit deeper and understand the difference between them, and how email can help.

Cross-sell

Cross-selling is promoting a product related to the original basket. This worked well in the Audible receipt example, with its, *"You might like these listens"* – a way to promote additional audiobooks.

You'll have seen this on Amazon, where it has a "People who bought this item also bought" box, displaying related items that go together. An example might be offering a bottle of orchid feed when someone buys an orchid.

For email marketing, this one can be a bit tricky, as your email platform will have to do the choosing of which products are related. If your email platform is connected to an online e-commerce store, it should be able to pull through products in the same category, so the choices shouldn't be too far out from the original.

For companies that only sell one thing or a big-ticket item, this kind of email is usually limited to accessories or extended warranties.

Upsell

This is offering the same product, but a larger or more expensive version. Imagine this as being a bigger plant, or a bigger pot that has more flowers in it.

In emails, this might be shown as, "Upgrade your 12 x Valentine's Roses bouquet to a bunch of 24 roses for only an extra £10", or, "Upgrade your ticket to first-class for free in-flight meals."

This is most commonly found in travel bookings or experiences (like the cinema), where you can upgrade your service ahead of getting there.

Most suitable for: Businesses selling more than one (related) thing online.

As an aside, some firms only sell one big ticket item, so the cross and upsells don't really apply. But it's important in this case to understand that people who buy the big-ticket item shouldn't then get email promotions trying to sell it to them.

REAL-WORLD EXAMPLE

I recently bought a reMarkable writing tablet as a way to try and keep my scribblings and email wireframes all in one place. It's got quite a hefty price tag and I'm only buying one – I wouldn't buy another one just yet! But about a week after purchasing (and a few weeks before it arrived), I got an email extoling the virtues of the product with a big, proud Buy Now button.

This is really easily solved for big-ticket sellers by grouping together customers in an email platform and making exclusions. I think reMarkable could group all the people who have bought in the last three years and set them to be excluded from 'acquisition' (the fancy way of saying new customers), because customers can only use one tablet at a time!

Replenishment reminder

Jess has bought her orchid and orchid feed, but if used properly, that bottle will be empty in three months.

Jess might be the super-organised type, measuring out the feed correctly, with the date on her calendar of when to re-order, but very few people have this Type A personality.

If we know that Jess is likely to run out of feed in three months' time, it makes sense to email her about two weeks before to remind her, giving her enough time to re-order and have it delivered.

These replenishment reminders work really well for non-perishable consumables, that is, things that last more than a month but run out within a year or so.

Examples of products that are ideally suited to this are: pet foods, plant food, baby powder, bike oil, toilet roll . . . the list goes on, and you're getting the picture.

Most suitable for: Businesses selling a consumable (it can be consumed and then run out) product.

Refer a friend

Word-of-mouth referral is the cornerstone of some businesses. It cuts through the noise, because a trusted friend is honestly relaying to you their experience and why it might be good for you. The business loses the control of the message a bit, but it's honest, genuine and people trust their friends' judgements (well, maybe not when it comes to, "Let's just have one more for the road" and a 3 am kebab).

Referrals are strong and they can be a powerful way to get new customers. But, as with reviews, people are predisposed to the negative rather than to positively referring business to you, so a gentle reminder can help them along.

Cash or a reward is a great incentive that a lot of businesses use. The RAC has a refer-a-friend email campaign, where the referrer and the new customer both get a £25 Marks and Spencer gift card. It certainly helps to get people who have had a good experience to get their friends signed up, and the double benefit to both parties is a win-win all round.

This example from Chroma Stationery gives both parties a £5 voucher to redeem against future purchases. This is a great way to increase more orders and, with some money off, customers tend to order just a little bit more than they otherwise might have done.

Most suitable for: B2C businesses

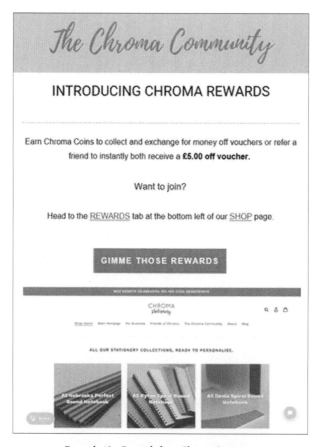

Example 43 – Rewards from Chroma Stationery.

Loyalty scheme/VIP membership club

Loyalty schemes can make for great email campaigns. They can push people off the fence into making another purchase where they might not have done so, and once you're in the 'club', the main aim is to increase repeat business through tiers, freebies and having an expiration date, or a shelf-life, to encourage even more purchases.

A monthly summary from Enterprise Rent-A-Car (See Example 44 over the page) details the number of rentals and Plus points in the account to be redeemed against future rentals, with a bonus double-points period.

A similar theme comes from the customised card company Moonpig, (See Example 45 over the page) which ran a "buy five cards and get your sixth card free" scheme.

This kind of prompting and clear communication can help customers fully understand the loyalty scheme, as well as encouraging ongoing and repeat purchases by setting birthday reminders.

A great way to embed a loyalty scheme is to have it present everywhere.

Subway's Subcard (while the point system is quite convoluted) makes a concerted effort to add in your points balance in the top of all their emails. (See Example 46 on page 195.)

Visualising this in terms of what the reward gets you can be a powerful cue in emails – like the Greggs Rewards section in the regular Greggs newsletter. Seeing I've bought three coffees and I'm just four more away from a free one can be super motivating and drive that extra little bit of performance for the business. (See Example 47 on page 195.)

Most suitable for: Businesses who sell consumables, or whose customers make regular purchases.

Example 44 & 45 – Enterprise receipt & Moonpig rewards.

Example 46 – Subway rewards.

Example 47– Greggs rewards.

Onboarding

This is a super important email sequence for a business that takes payment on a regular basis, or for something that's quite complex to set up and transition to using regularly, but most businesses wouldn't necessarily need one, which is why I've included it lower down the list.

It's like a welcome sequence (that we covered in the Saying Hello section), but instead of welcoming a new subscriber with a view to making a sale, we're welcoming a new customer with a view to keeping their continued business.

The main aim of the onboarding sequence is to reduce churn (the people who cancel), by making sure as many questions are answered as possible and the customers are feeling satisfied.

This can be a standalone sequence, but it will often incorporate bits of the different emails detailed in this section.

Let's look at an example for a three-wave onboarding campaign for a monthly "Plants by Post" subscription box from Poppy's Plants. The box costs £29.99 a month and has a bunch of easily transportable plants all ready to adorn customers' houses:

Email #1 - About this email:

→ Sent just after the receipt, the main aim is to explain what's happening.

Onboarding campaign example from Poppy's Plants - Step 1	
To:	Jess Reader
From:	Poppy's Plants by Post
Subject line:	You're in the Plants by Post club!
Preview text:	A warm welcome.
Email content:	Hi Jess, Thanks for joining Plants by Post, you've made a great decision. Every month, you'll get a box in the post (it'll fit through your letterbox, so it won't matter if you're not in) with gorgeous seasonal plants and flowers that will decorate any sized home. They're guaranteed for three weeks (and almost always last longer in good light and with regular watering). Here are a few photos from happy customers: [Instagram images from customers]

Onboarding campaign example from Poppy's Plants – Step 1	
Email Content:	Now you're in, let's get down to it – what happens next? 1. You get this email saying hello! 2. We'll post out your box today (or the next working day if it's a weekend). 3. We'll post out your next box a month from today, and every month on the 18th. We all need a break sometimes, and if you're away or want to pause your box, just log into your member account and click 'Pause'. Just make sure to pause it three working days before the 18th of every month, otherwise you might still be charged. I'm Poppy and I want you to be totally happy and satisfied with your plants. If you have any problems with any of your orders or any questions, feel free to email me personally at poppy@poppysplants.co.uk, or call the shop on 0117 555 0123. Happy planting, Poppy

Email #2 - About this email:

→ A week after the first box was put in the post – similar to the shipment check-in email.

Onboarding campaign example from Poppy's Plants - Step 2	
To:	Jess Reader
From:	Poppy's Plants by Post
Subject line:	How did you get on with your first box?
Preview text:	Just checking in.
Email content:	Hi Jess, I'm just checking in to see how you got on with your first Plants by Post box. The care instructions are in the box, but if you're not sure about something or it's looking a bit off, please do get in touch and I can help. If you've got any queries or feedback, please let me know. Until next month! Happy planting, Poppy

Email #3 - About this email:

→ Three weeks after the first box was put in the post – this is a pre-renewal email, with the main aim of making the reader aware they're about to be charged and also give them some social proof that others loved their boxes. It also gives a useful reminder on how to log in and the key dispatch times.

Onboarding campaign example from Poppy's Plants - Step 3	
To:	Jess Reader
From:	Poppy's Plants by Post
Subject line:	Why our customers love Plants by Post.
Preview text:	"It's just so easy to have seasonal plants delivered!"
Email content:	Hi Jess,
	These last few weeks have flown by, and I hope you've enjoyed this month's box.
	We've had some great feedback from our happy customers:
	"Love these! They make our house a home!"
	"This is a fab idea. I know nothing about plants, so it makes me look great when I have dinner parties."
	"Having seasonal plants delivered makes everything so much easier."

Onboarding campaign example from Poppy's Plants - Step 3	
Email content:	Just to remind you, your next box will be dispatched on the 18th, so if you want to make any changes, like choosing a different selection of flowers or skipping the next month, just log into your account and make the changes by the 15th. If you have any problems or questions, please get in touch. Happy planting, Poppy

Most suitable for: Memberships and subscriptions – these tend to be businesses who sell something that's billed monthly or annually, like software, mobile phone tariffs, postal subscription boxes and insurance companies.

Non-recent customers

I've put this one last for a reason: the businesses that will have the email permission to get in touch with a customer who made a historic purchase and yet haven't followed up with them since will be few and far between.

Getting a new customer can cost five times more than keeping an existing one, and if there's a (properly permissioned!) email list of previous customers that haven't been reached out to for a while then why not get in touch?

Previous customers bought from you for a reason, and they're much more likely to do business with you again.

For Poppy's Plants, this might be an audit every six months, to find out who they haven't reached out to in a while.

It might just be a more customer-services based, "I saw you bought a large indoor plant from us two years ago. How is it and is there anything you need?"

Or it could be more promotional. "You bought from us two years ago, so I'm just checking in to see if there's anything else you need. We've got 30% off our new orchids that you might enjoy."

Most suitable for: Well-established businesses with a list of previous customers.

Don't let the purchase confirmation be the last thing your new customers see. Keep them updated and happy, and long may they continue to be repeat customers!

Action to do now:

→ Plan out how customers buy and what they receive (across email, SMS, postal, paper receipt). Then look back at a few of the examples we've covered, incorporating any that you think will fit your business model.

WRAPPING IT UP

Phew! We're at the end of converting more readers, one of the hardest things to get right. Setting up an email list and getting people on it is relatively straightforward. But putting in the effort and hours to consistently show up with the right message at the right time, with a view to help lighten the reader's wallet a little, is more of an art than a science, and using what you've learned, it's time for you to think about how you can apply it in your business.

We've covered:

- ✓ What data is and how to make sure you stay legal.

- ✓ Why it's super important to have data about your readers, with some examples of how to maximise it.

- ✓ How to identify and get rid of duff subscribers who don't open your emails.

- ✓ What segmentation and personalisation is, and why it's important to building relationships using email.

- ✓ How to use automated emails to boost conversions and sales.

- ✓ The plethora of emails you could use post-purchase to keep new customers happy and content.

You'll get some of it wrong, especially as you start out. You won't get sales from the very first email send. Stick with it. Look at what worked well, what bombed and find out how to *Send Better Emails* for your audience and your business.

Putting it all together

So, we've covered a lot:

- ✓ How to build a strategy, plan emails out and define our success metrics.
- ✓ How to grow an audience, get them to sign up, welcome new readers and promote the list.
- ✓ How to turn readers into customers using data, working smarter with automations and post-purchase sequences.

In this final chapter, we're going to bring it all together with our Poppy's Plants examples, imagining we're starting out from the very beginning and planning out what we need to do to get going and then what would be nice to look at going forward.

We all start out with zero subscribers, which might seem daunting, as I thought when I looked forlornly at an empty Word document when I first started writing this book. But with hard work and determination, it does get better.

Let's imagine Poppy's Plants has been on the high street for a few years. While they've got an e-commerce website that does OK, it doesn't generate that many sales.

The main goal is to build a subscriber base and increase the number of orders coming through the website.

Starting from zero

Let's focus on what basic email sequence you should start with. As you get more confident, you can implement all of the bells and whistles that I've explained in previous chapters.

If you don't have a website or store at all, I'd recommend the MailChimp (email platform), WordPress (website) and WooCommerce (e-commerce provider) trio, as they're easy to get going and cheap to maintain.

I'm not going to cover anything new in this chapter, it's a summary of everything from the book so far, incorporating an example from start to finish. I've left out the more ambitious elements like Power Ups, but head back to the relevant sections to learn more.

Pick your platform

There are over four hundred email platforms that you can choose from. But which one's right for you? As you're starting out from zero, I'll always recommend MailChimp.

It's the easiest to set up and gives more flexibility as you scale up. I'm a MailChimp partner and I honestly believe it's the best choice to get started with, no matter what your business model might be.

There are a few others worthy of consideration: Drip for its automation sequences, Keap for being more of a business system you can keep client data in, Klaviyo if SMS marketing is something you want to explore.

Whatever you pick, think about whether it will fit your needs in six months' time. I recommend MailChimp because you can add in re-targeted paid advertising campaigns, Facebook, Google and Instagram adverts and even postcards. The customer automation journeys are really easy to use and understand, making it a great fit for a range of businesses.

Price wise, there is a free option, but only for sending newsletters. As we want to make some money, we'll be wanting the automations, which start from £10/month for 500 contacts, going up incrementally the more contacts you have.

Email as a marketing channel has a great return on investment. You'll see tons of stats banded about the internet that it's about 42x (that means for every £1 you spend, you get £42 back in revenue), and that's accurate if you refer to *Send Better Emails* and follow the advice – it's not osmosis, and just reading this won't get you more sales.

Paying for an email platform should never be lost money and should always turn a profit (although this might not happen in the first few months of getting started).

So, going back to Poppy's Plants, let's assume she signs up for the £10/month Standard MailChimp plan. Even if she sells one item, this means it has paid for itself. And ideally, she'll sell a lot more.

Data

Before we open up our email platform, we need to plan out what pieces of information (data) we want to know about people. These can include:

→ **First Name**

This is a great place to start, and it will help us personalise emails with "Hello Jess."

→ **Email address**

We obviously need to know the right address to send the email.

→ **Birthday**

This is a great nugget to help us offer birthday rewards.

Poppy's Plants is just setting up their email platform, so we'll just stick to first name, email and birthday. In previous chapters, we talked about more advanced plans, such as offering choices to help promote more relevant products (like indoor or outdoor plants), but this is starting from zero, so let's keep it simple.

E-commerce

As Poppy's Plants already has an e-commerce site, it will be helpful to connect the website to the email platform (this is why I recommend the MailChimp/WooCommerce combo, because the integration is really easy).

Doing this can help us promote the right product and also follow up with customers that start the purchase process but don't get all the way to the end.

Creating a newsletter

And finally, but by no means least important, it's time to set up the newsletter.

"Plant Care" goes out every fortnight and has a featured product, some plant care tips, a video and some related interior decoration that's plant focused.

As we're starting out, it's likely the number of subscribers is zero, but that doesn't mean we shouldn't ask current customers what they might want to see in a newsletter. The ideas that come from customers can really help open our eyes to what the people want and, ultimately, that's the main goal of all content-based marketing.

It's helpful to create a template in the email platform, so the wheel isn't being reinvented every time. This investment in getting it to exactly how we want it to look and then duplicating it for future campaigns helps us to keep the focus where it should be: on the content. Nobody wants to be resetting the fonts the day before a newsletter is due out.

Readers can sign up to the newsletter through the popups or on the homepage. Social media pages can also link directly to the newsletter sign up, and this can be promoted on those pages.

Starting the newsletter from scratch means it can be a bit of a work in progress. Don't aim for perfection, aim for done. The next task can be to build on it and make it even better.

A newsletter is a really easy place to get started. Now, let's look at the automations Poppy's Plants might want to use.

Sign ups: Lead magnets

Poppy's Plants needs to sign up website visitors to become email readers. The first thing to do is to add in a non-invasive popup form. (Go back if you want to check out the examples on how not to do it!)

The main offer on the popup form and in adverts across the website will be two lead magnets, so readers are enticed to type in their email addresses.

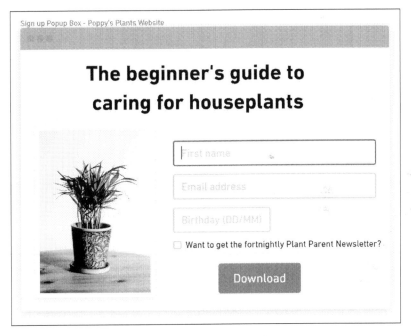

Example 48 – Lead magnet sign-up form.

Using Beacon (sendbetter.email/beacon), they create two free downloads:

→ **The beginner's guide to caring for houseplants**

This is aimed at readers at the starting point, who are interested in dipping their toes into the houseplant world. They might be interested in a "Houseplant Starter Kit" comprising four plants with pots, food and a mini watering calendar.

→ **The complete list of plants that are hard to kill**

This guide is aimed at readers who think houseplants aren't for them, and it recommends a range of cacti and succulents that are easy to care for.

On the sidebar in blog posts and on the website homepage, both free downloads are offered, so readers can enter their email address to download the guide.

The email flow looks quite similar, although with different content (see the email flowchart 4 on the next page).

→ **Email 1** gives the reader what they asked for: a link to the download.

→ **Email 2** is a follow up a day later, asking if the reader has any more questions and providing some product recommendations related to the downloaded guide.

→ **Email 3** offers a 15% off discount code on a specific product or type of product, to try and tempt the reader into becoming a customer.

At this point, the email platform connects to the e-commerce website and checks if the free download or the follow-up email has converted the reader into a customer.

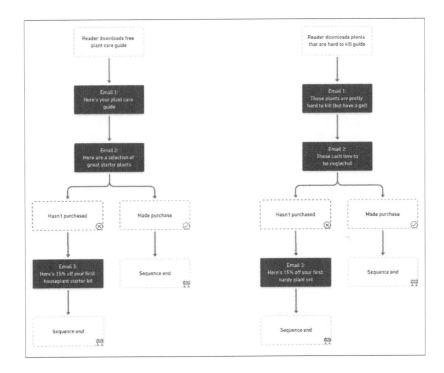

Email flowchart 4 – Example lead magnets to increase sales and reduce cannibalistic discounting.

If it has, job done, drinks all round.

If not, let's see if a discount code might push the reader over the edge.

Coupons and discounts

A word on coupons and discounts: the main reason there is a "has purchased?" check between emails two and three is to avoid 'coupon resentment', where a non-discounted purchase is made, and then a customer gets a coupon and ends up feeling like a mug for buying at full price.

This can be really irritating – I recently renewed my Adobe Creative Cloud subscription (I used to teach InDesign and Photoshop some years ago, and I still use it quite regularly). About a month after being charged quite a hefty subscription price, I received an email offering me a £150 Amazon voucher if I bought a subscription. These kind of purchase checks are available in most email platforms, and it's vital to avoid this kind of coupon resentment.

Automations

Three easy-to-launch email sequences

1. Hello/Welcome

When readers tick the "Sign up to the Plant Care newsletter", we want to send them a simple, three-email sequence welcome.

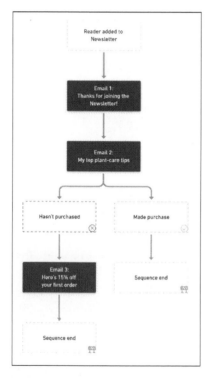

Email flowchart 5 – An example welcome sequence.

→ **Email 1** will focus on introducing the brand and thanking the reader for joining the newsletter.

→ **Email 2** will feature some of the most read blogs and videos, as a way to drive more traffic to the website.

Then, similar to the previous campaigns, there will be checks to see if a purchase has been made and, if not, Email 3 will be sent, which contains a discount code.

This is why connecting your e-commerce site to your email platform is so important – it can help drive the right people down the right paths in the flowchart.

Why you'd use this: Welcome sequences get readers in the habit of seeing your name on their screen and clicking open. It's also now very common, so it's mostly about keeping up!

2. Happy Birthday

If readers give their birthday, email platforms can work their magic and set automatic birthday email campaigns to go out. This is a 'set and forget' type campaign, although I must stress that you shouldn't forget about it completely – make sure you check it every now and again to make sure all the content is relevant and up to date. See email flowchart number 6 on the following page.

The best birthday loyalty and retention campaigns have a small free giveaway, as opposed to a discount code, as you can frame it as "Claim your free birthday gift."

Think of the Subway free cookie example or Pizza Express's free bottle of Prosecco from earlier. I know of a few large brands that have used a small £3 Costa Coffee/Starbucks e-gift card to great success. The idea of 'surprise and delight' goes over really well.

→ **Email 1:** (7 days before birthday) It's almost your birthday, treat yourself.

→ **Email 2:** (On birthday, preferably first thing in the morning) Happy birthday, Jess!

Again, there should be a purchase check to see if the coupon/freebie was redeemed and if not, send Email 3: (3 days post-birthday) Don't forget to claim your birthday gift!

Why you'd use this: It costs several magnitudes more to get a new customer than it does to keep existing ones loyal. A low-cost freebie? Improves the customer's Lifetime Value (from Section One – Chapter 3: *Defining Success*).

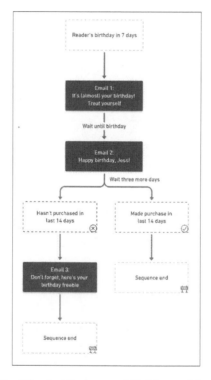

Email flowchart 6 – An example birthday email flow.

3. Abandoned basket

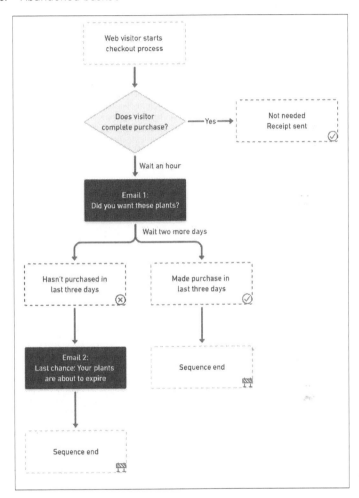

Email flowchart 7 – An abandoned-basket sequence.

If you use MailChimp and WooCommerce, this can take a few clicks to set up, but as with most email platforms, it's still pretty straightforward.

Connecting your e-commerce site with your email platform means they share data – so, if someone gets halfway through the checkout and drops out, the basket has been 'abandoned' and we can follow up with a gentle reminder.

There's a school of thought that says this is a campaign you should stuff with discounts, but this can reward bad discount-hunting behaviour, where customers become trained never to pay full price.

This is totally up to you and what makes most sense for your brand, but if a customer got as far as adding to the basket and working their way through typing in their details, I would argue it's more likely they got interrupted and switched task rather than getting halfway through a process just to maybe get a coupon.

→ **Email 1**: (Sent shortly after/an hour after website visit) We saved your basket. Very simple, click back to checkout.

Another purchase check – There's nothing worse than following up on a transaction that's already gone through.

→ **Email 2**: (Sent two days later) Last chance: Your plants/basket is about to expire.

Why you'd use this: This campaign gives you a second bite at the e-commerce apple, and it's useful for those selling products that customers buy on site.

The post-purchase experience

The email activity has started converting readers into customers – hurray! But let's also quickly consider what happens after the till goes cha-ching.

This example is for Poppy's Plants orders delivered by post, but it can be altered to your purchase setup:

Email flowchart 8 – A post-purchase email sequence.

→ **Email 1**: (Instantly) Receipt or order confirmation.

→ **Email 2**: (Once order is marked as dispatched in your e-commerce site) Your order is on the way.

→ **Email 3**: (Once order is delivered, or after a week) Your order has been delivered, let us know of any defects, problems or issues.

→ **Email 4**: (One day later) How to care for your plant. Here, it might be a list of links to the various plant-care guides on your website, as we're starting out simple here.

→ **Email 5**: (One week later) Was everything OK? Write us a review on Trustpilot/Google.

→ **Email 6**: (Another ten weeks later) It's been three months – how are you getting on?

Why you'd want to do this: Takes care of customers' main queries on autopilot. They want to be kept updated, and again, linking our e-commerce and email platforms saves the day in communicating order statuses.

The last thought

And that's a whistle-stop tour of how Poppy's Plants would start from zero. Even if you've got a different business model, you should be able to see what we're trying to do and emulate it to fit your situation.

Start with picking a platform, get the sign ups sorted, send a newsletter and then sort out the easy automations.

Glossary

A/B test

Sending two versions of an email to an audience, with the aim of improving performance by learning something. This might be "Does adding emojis in my subject line improve the open rate?" More learning resources on A/B testing in email can be found at junction.email

Automated email

An email sent because a reader has done something, like downloaded an eBook or made a purchase. This email is set up once and then just needs occasionally checking on.

Click through rate (CTR)

The percentage of readers who received an email and then clicked a link. This can be modified by the open rate, so I recommend using the CTOR instead.

Click to open rate (CTOR)

The percentage of readers who opened an email and then clicked a link. This is a more accurate number to use because it is a better reflection of how good the content is. I recommend using this metric when calculating clicks.

Email campaign

A one-off email sent to your audience, like a newsletter or a timely discount or sale.

Email client

The program your reader uses to view their emails. Common examples include Gmail, Outlook and Webmail. You can find the latest percentages at EmailClientMarketShare.com.

Email platform

A software used to send emails to your readers. I recommend using MailChimp.

Email programme

A term used to talk about the whole sum of all campaigns and automations. This usually includes every marketing email sent by a company.

Open rate

The percentage of readers who received your email and then opened it. This is known by email platforms adding in an invisible image, but this metric can be unreliable for those with a high number of readers using Outlook or blocking images.

Popup

A box that displays on a website asking for an email address, with the intention to sign up to a mailing list.

Spam complaint

When a reader didn't sign up to receive an email, they can click a button that says, "Mark as Spam". If you get a lot of these, it can mean you get labelled a spammer.

Unsubscribe

When a reader doesn't want to get an email anymore, they can click an unsubscribe link to request they be removed from the mailing list.

Reference

Bendle N., Ferris P., et al. (2020), *Marketing Metrics: The Definitive Guide to Measuring Marketing Performance*, Pearson FT Press

Kahavi R., Tang D. and Xu Y. (2020), *Trustworthy Online Controlled Experiments: A Practical Guide to A/B Testing*, Cambridge University Press

Thomas B. (2013), *Watertight Marketing (1st Edition)*, Panoma Press

Thomas B. (2020), *Watertight Marketing (2nd Edition)*, Human Business Thinking

Vaynerchuk G. (2018), *Crushing It!*, Harper Business

About the author

Jon May is an email marketing expert with Inbox Hero. He works with companies large and small, from the RAC and global franchises, to a national mobility retail store chain, and all the way down to individuals starting their own business.

He studied marketing at Swansea University, taught journalism for a bit, managed a marketing department for a London university and then set up his own business in marketing training and consultancy. After a while, Jon focused and 'niched' down into email marketing, to great success.

Jon is a little obsessed with email. After a full day's work helping companies on their email marketing, he likes to relax by working at The Email Research Lab™ (emailresearch.io) on an array of technical, strategic and analytical tools to make the email marketing industry better.

In his spare time, Jon likes to tend to his large and varied indoor plant collection, take out his electric bike and cook and bake (pies are a favourite).

You can find Jon tweeting witty, email-related one-liners at @JonDoesEmails, read his blog at sendbetter.email/blog or email him about email (very meta!) at jon@inboxhero.co.uk.

Acknowledgements

I don't want this to sound like a cliché Oscar acceptance speech, but I didn't do the work in this book and my learning leading up to it all by myself.

To my best friends, Molly, Jake and Sam. Great friends, confidants and drinking partners. Words can't describe the depth of my gratitude for the support you've shown me, especially when I start on about emails and you fight the need to take an immediate and unscheduled nap.

I'd like to thank my dad for teaching me HTML back in the '90s, when I was just a wee bairn. We had a Windows 95 PC with a dial-up modem, and I can still hear my mum screeching through the house: "Get off the internet, I need to make a call!"

My dad was a big embracer of the early web and launched his own website jokemaster.com of hand-drawn illustrated jokes sketched in Coral and Paint. My favourite joke was, "A balanced diet is a bacon sandwich in each hand!"

It's easy nowadays to get started with a website, but this was in the days before WordPress. You had to code each page. BY HAND. Then upload them to a server and hope nothing went wonky.

Being the curious kid I was, my dad (very patiently) taught me how to build web pages with all the tags you need <head><body><img> and the like, as well as the technical bits and bobs to get a website going.

Email platforms have advanced at warp speed, but the core HTML that email programs like Outlook and Gmail use hasn't. Quite a bit of it is still stuck in the '90s. So, when I started working in HTML for emails, I was right at home. I was transported back to my childhood dining room, where there was an enormous tower and cube monitor display, Britney Spears played on the radio and the internet was a really small place. I chose to go into emails mostly because of this skill, and I'm incredibly grateful to have had the ten-year head start.

I'd like to thank my grandparents for their help in getting my business up and running, as well as this book being published. They provided a dedicated office space, where I could start out as a bright-eyed twenty-something with a vision to make marketing better, and granny's lunches kept me going.

My grandparents have been great cheerleaders, enthusiastically sitting through my tediously dull webinars on very niche areas in email marketing, like the process of churning out nice looking emails in big businesses and how emails can support membership-based organisations.

They've been very helpful in taking in parcels, letting me run a business from their home office and keeping me on task to finish this book.

I must say a huge thank you to all the entrepreneurs and staff at the NatWest Entrepreneurship Accelerator. Steve, Helen, Charly, Andy, Heidi, Kieran – the list goes on. Thank you so much. From forcing me to perform my pitch on-the-spot, to helping me refine my ideas to be slightly less sh*t, it was an honour and a privilege to work alongside this bunch of inspirational people that are going places.

And to Kay, the lady who taught me how to write properly. She was my journalism tutor/mentor from my time working on the university newspaper, and we've been great friends ever since. I remember when I first started as a lowly student journalist, Kay used to crack out the red pen for corrections – trying to undo the damage a state education does to your writing skills. But the more she sent back, the better my writing became, and eventually, I hope, it's blossomed into something readable.

To the #EmailGeeks community of 10k email marketers for answering my questions. Hopefully, I've given more back than I've taken! There are a few outstanding email marketers that have really been an inspiration in my career: Elliot Ross (superb DJ), Kitty Bates, Jay Oram, Paul Airy, Andrew and Nely Bonar, April Mullen and Stephanie Griffith, the last of whom has saved me weeks of time with her emailpreview.io tool to download emails as images. I could mention more people, but this book has to end sometime, so I better wrap it up.